HANS HOLZER'S

THE
SUPERNATURAL

EXPLAINING
THE UNEXPLAINED

HANS HOLZER'S

THE SUPERNATURAL

EXPLAINING THE UNEXPLAINED

New Page Books
A division of The Career Press, Inc.
Franklin Lakes, NJ

HANS HOLZER'S THE SUPERNATURAL
EDITED AND TYPESET BY CLAYTON W. LEADBETTER
Cover design by Cheryl Cohan Finbow
Printed in the U.S.A. by Book-mart Press

To order this title, please call toll-free 1-800-CAREER-1 (NJ and Canada: 201-848-0310) to order using VISA or MasterCard, or for further information on books from Career Press.

The Career Press, Inc., 3 Tice Road, PO Box 687,
Franklin Lakes, NJ 07417
www.careerpress.com
www.newpagebooks.com

Library of Congress Cataloging-in-Publication Data

Holzer, Hans.
    Hans Holzer's the supernatural : explaining the unexplained / by
Hans Holzer.
        p. cm.
    Includes index.
    ISBN 1-56414-661-8 (pbk.)
        1. Parapsychology. 2. Supernatural. I. Title: Supernatural. II. Title.

BF1031.H672 2003
133--dc21

2003044572

FEAR
is the absence of
KNOWLEDGE.

CONTENTS

FOREWORD

One fine day some years ago, I was walking on a California beach road with the late Bishop James Pike, erstwhile bishop of California, talking about a subject that interested us both: true experiences and phenomena that seemingly lay outside the recognized boundaries of modern science. I am a parapsychologist and author, and Jim took issue with the term "parapsychology," a term created by Professor Joseph B. Rhine for the study of anything that was at present outside the realm of psychology.

"If it is real, then it belongs into psychology," he intoned, "and if the boundaries of modern psychology cannot accommodate these events, then the boundaries need to be adjusted to include the phenomena currently dealt with by parapsychology."

Science is merely a quest for knowledge, not ultimate knowledge itself. Regrettably, most scientists stay "with the book," that is, feel secure only by sticking to what they have been taught by their teachers back in school—from middle to university. But going by the book is incomplete and often false, because newer discoveries have replaced earlier notions of the same subject.

Most dangerous of all, personal bias, beliefs, and disbeliefs enter the conclusions of scientists and tend to cause false results in their thinking or conclusions. Thus, when we speak of the "supernatural" we are using a term the conventional scientist or observer would use, because the matters falling into the realm of what we here call the "supernatural" are in fact perfectly natural; they are just outside the traditional, conservative view of the universe—a view arrived at a long time ago and not really brought up to date.

But there is nothing, nothing whatever in our world that is not truly natural, because it exists and can be studied. Cartesius stated long ago, "Cogito, ergo sum," which has been incorrectly translated as "I think, therefore I am," when in the French of his time, the actual meaning was, "As I think, so I am."

By the time this book has become part of your consciousness, you will have realized that yesterday's *supernatural* is today and tomorrow's *natural*. This is a no-nonsense book, clearing up misconceptions and calling things by their proper names and avoiding anything based only on belief, disbelief, or religious or quasi-religious ideas. I will also be taking on the sense and nonsense of channeling, as well as mediumship, both genuine and the kind you get with a 900-number phone call, and the use of such implements and psychic aids as Ouija boards, cards, and crystal balls.

The approach will be open-minded and definitely frank, not based on any preconceived notions, but on hard evidence, no matter how strange some of that evidence may seem to people not familiar with the way evidence is obtained.

In the end, the *supernatural* is that portion of the natural world we will all fully understand some day not too distant in the future.

Here is a book giving you advance information with practical applications for *now*.

—Professor Hans Holzer, Ph.D.

INTRODUCTION

BODY, MIND, AND SPIRIT: THE TRIPLE NATURE OF MANKIND

If we accept the physical aspects of human existence, and there cannot possibly be any doubt about that, we will have to explain to our satisfaction the nonphysical aspects of our lives as well. Even today there are medical people—those dealing with the mind as well as those dealing in physiology—who will fight any notion that everything about mankind cannot be explained satisfactorily from the purely physical point of view.

In fact, even some parapsychologists have avoided accepting the notion of another dimension—a nonphysical world—which is the home of psychic phenomena, and a connecting link for communications purporting to come from such a dimension. From this perspective, everything a psychically gifted person does in the way of receiving and presenting phenomena must therefore be explained on the basis that such phenomena originate in man's physical body and organs, all of it falling well within the conventional view of human existence.

Any attempt to extend the source of that origination into areas generally dealt with by religion (or metaphysics, religion's lesser brother) is considered strictly outside scientific inquiry of any kind, and properly dealt with by religion and, at best, metaphysics, which have nothing whatever to do with science and scientific research. But the evidence lies elsewhere, and once the phenomena are looked at dispassionately and carefully, yes, even scientifically, it becomes abundantly clear that the physical body per se cannot, within the boundaries of conventional medical and scientific knowledge of the same, produce them.

It has long been known that man is both a physical entity and something else, and as parapsychology made progress, we have been able to give hard evidence of that inner body, the etheric, seat of human personality, which leaves the physical outer shell at death, and proceeds to a parallel world in which it continues to function fully without the limitations of a heavier, physical body. Obviously then, we are dealing with the two separate aspects of life, joined together temporarily while on the physical plane of existence.

If the universal law of physics and chemistry is a firm basis for the development of all things physical in the universe following scientifically valid and immutable rules, then the spiritual law of the universe must do the same for the other component of life—human, animal, plant—also according to firm and immutable rules. But the spiritual side of man is also emotional, and therefore the spiritual law must deal with a value system involving the emotions, actions, and other individual elements, and in this respect it is more complex than the law governing the material universe. There is nothing haphazard about this, of course, even though each human individual will be considered by the law individually, yet by the same overall standards and concepts.

Now we can accept the slow development of the physical universe quasi by itself on the basis of what we know about the laws of physics and chemistry. But when it comes to the spiritual law, we are confronted by some fundamental questions. The first one of these is easy to answer. If this spiritual law exists—and it does—and if it evaluates humans individually as to their spiritual development and actions, some sort of staff, some sort of bureaucracy is required to do this work.

The evidence is firm and multifaceted that people who pass from this physical life into the next stage of life, the etheric dimension, or if you like, the "spirit world," are not sitting around twiddling their etheric thumbs for eternity either. As I understand it from countless investigations, everybody works. Unlike our American welfare system, anyone who can contribute to administering the system is placed into a position of responsibility appropriate for the individual's skill, intelligence, and development—all of which pass untouched from the physical world into the next.

This of course still leaves unanswered the twin questions of "Who is the boss?" and "Who put him there?" For the moment, let us refer here to *God* the way we often refer to *the government*, without naming individuals, but rather a principle, a power, an authority. As to who put him there, and what was there before his time, that is pure three-dimensional thinking. In the world of spirit, we do not have conventional time and space, but rather an eternal now, a continuum that flows and never stops.

Lest you consider such notions as purely metaphysical, they are not. Albert Einstein has stated that, at the subatomic level, time and space are interchangeable. Our concept of time and space is appropriate for our finite world, our finite physical life spans, and our local environment. But common sense would indicate that other inhabited planets in other solar systems would go by their own appropriate time-space continuum, not ours. Time and space concepts, then, depend largely on the physical world they refer to and regulate. That physical world will differ greatly, one from the next, because different planets in different galaxies have different distances from their life-giving sun, and thus different living conditions. These very real conditions determine the *space factor* for each world. The *time factor*, on the other hand, is connected with the relative age of the planet, that is, for how long a period the particular planet has been subjected to the natural influences—physical and chemical—that are the natural, primary forces of the universe responsible for all development from formation of the planet to the beginning of life on it.

Now it is probably not difficult to accept and even understand the workings of nature that lead to man's existence on this particular world, Earth, in respect to his physical, material self. But we know there is another side to man, a different set of laws, the spiritual side. Here is where man goes astray more often than not, because he is confronted with a system that does not go by the same safe rules as the system regarding the physical, material world within which he is more comfortable. To begin with, the facts are much harder to pin down. What exactly is the other, spiritual side of man? Can we measure it, separate it at death from the dying body? How do the two sides of man interrelate to form the whole?

Man never doubted the existence of that spiritual component from the very beginning of human existence. Even the cave dweller turned to the shaman to handle that side of things. The spiritual side also became a repository of anything man could not explain on purely material grounds. The paranormal, the seeming miracles, the ability to reach human beings across distances by thought alone, all of these man knew very early on, but he neither could nor wanted to know how they worked and why. Instead, he turned all that over to the shaman, thus creating a power position for one man, which, in the wrong hands, could be dangerous indeed.

To make things even more complicated, early man had no explanation for most natural occurrences, from lightning to storms, from rainbows to earthquakes, from bad luck to good fortune, from illness to fear. These happenings thus became the province of the supernatural, a world populated by a variety of deities, none of whom early man ever got to see directly.

Now the laws of the physical universe continue indefinitely to shape all that is in that universe affecting, of course, man's own development of body and mind across this world's time-space continuum. Caveman becomes civilized man and civilized man discovers history and acts in it. With his physical skills and his developing mind, man discovers more and more about himself, his environment, and his potential; and as he does, his desires also increase, and expansion of one kind or another occurs.

But what about the spiritual side of man? The early shaman has long yielded to the priest, the gods have gotten more defined and have been given certain human traits so that common man might better understand and relate to them. The priest defines the system of a supposed invisible world populated by a variety of supernatural entities, and religion becomes a fact of life.

Man is happy to hear that now all he has to do is join a group and go by the rules the priest has set forth. The result should certainly be a give and take relationship between him and the deities. Some things he wants, he will get—if the deities decide favorably—and some things he won't. It is a comfort for man to have deferred his curiosity about his own spirituality to the supernatural world and to have that reliable spokesman, the priest, to answer all questions.

But it is not long before temporal rules of a developing Earth discover another side to the emergence of organized religion. Whoever controls the particular religion most favored by their people, also controls the people.

The scientific approach to research in parapsychology is pretty well established. Laboratory re-creations and artificial conditions used to get positive results from gifted psychic individuals—long the mainstay of research originated by the late Professor Joseph Banks Rhine at Duke University in the 1930s—have yielded more and more to competent field research and the observation, correlation, and analysis of observed and witnessed phenomena when they occur naturally and, usually, unexpectedly.

The enormous body of evidence regarding three types of naturally occurring phenomena cannot possibly be explained away by tortured and mostly unproven alternate explanations. They are:

1. The observed apparitions of people after their physical deaths.
2. The direct auditory experiences of witnesses in respect to departed people.
3. Communications, either directly or through competent and reputable intermediaries, mediums, or psychics, that can only come from the claimant in the world of spirit.

To the skeptic, there simply *must* be another explanation for this, one that fits within the framework of current scientific thinking—and limitations. In other words, what the skeptic is looking for is a way out of having to accept the existence of a spiritual continuity after death, one in which our persona seems totally intact, and even happy.

The arguments put forth by skeptics—usually without any regard to actual details of individual cases—are that the perception of an apparition of a loved one after death must be due to grief, or if there is no personal emotional connection, and it is a total stranger whose spirit has appeared to a witness, the witness must be hallucinating and should see a psychiatrist.

We had a fair number of authentic photographs taken under scientific test conditions showing figures of spirits, people on the Other Side of Life, proving of course that their etheric bodies, which they now inhabit, are not exactly made of nothing, but of a finer substance, similar to the relationship between a heavy tire (the physical body) and its inner tube (the etheric body).

But in order to understand the real nature of the spiritual system, you should fully understand the reality of that other dimension—

and not simply believe. Belief or disbelief have nothing to do with the evidence, and the evidence alone—not emotional leanings—should allow one to accept the existence of that other world, so close to this one.

No doubt about it, religion—any religion—has had an enormous influence on mankind from very early times. It supplied to the average man an edifice that gave him comfort and explained things he could not readily understand about the universe and some aspects of his own nature. But religion is also responsible for the greatest tragedies in the development of mankind. More people have been killed for the sake of religion of one kind or another, than for any other cause. Second to it is fanatical nationalism, but this ranks far, far behind religion. This holds true for all religions, but Christianity particularly must bear its share of guilt for having allowed so much cruelty and destruction to occur in its name.

Even at the outset, when Christianity had just become the official Roman State religion, hundreds of thousands died because of a dispute between two interpreters of Jesus' teachings. Was he divinely inspired, and a man, as Arianus preached, or was he literally God's son, as Athanasius would have it? The Roman State preferred Athanasius' version because it helped them build a stronger power base, bearing in mind that Pagan religion was far from dead throughout the ancient world. The Egyptian trinity of Horus, Osiris, and Isis suggested a Christian counterpart in God the Father, God the Son (Jesus), and the Virgin Mary. The latter was shortly pronounced to be beyond human laws so that the Immaculate Conception of Jesus could be matched by the Virgin Birth. Now the holy trinity was complete, and people responded to it positively for centuries to come.

Over the years, and through countless interpretations and rewrites of Holy Scriptures, Jesus became more and more assimilated with God the Father, and to this day, among American fundamentalists, the distinction is not even very clear. The Essene prophet Jesus, the gentle reformer, the divinely inspired potential savior, vanished in the process.

The word of God is not totally lost in all religions by any means. It is sometimes diluted, sometimes misinterpreted, or sometimes made conditional upon a kind of loyalty oath of sticking to the ground rules of that particular faith.

More and more, over the centuries, man seems to have forgotten that, according to the Scriptures, "God created man in his image." Instead, man seems to have created God in his image. This, of course, is what the ancients did with their often very human pantheon of gods. It was both comfortable and presented many aspects of the one and only true deity, which even the ancients realized.

So who is in charge? And who put him (her?) in charge? That, of course, is purely the reasoning of the physical world. And from a physical point of view it is difficult to understand that an entirely different set of laws operates the spiritual system.

"God" simply is; no time or space is involved in a dimension that knows neither. We know for a fact now that spiritual dimension exists, based not on faith or religious conviction, but available evidence. But a spiritual universe, especially one so well organized and administered, surely must have an intelligence in charge of it, just as the physical universe has authorities.

As mentioned earlier, referring to God, it is a little like saying "the government," which does not mean any particular person in the government, but its power, its principle. So it is, I feel, with God. I use the word *God* to mean the creative power that permeates the spiritual universe, and its highest expression.

There is an entire cottage industry comprised of angel lore, which even includes at least one newsletter. Why would a human figure, male or female, with two arms and two legs, need a couple of wings to fly? Anatomically, this is absurd. Birds have wings because they don't have arms. Besides, whenever spirits, even guides, have appeared to people in this dimension, they glide about effortlessly, and when they leave, they "fly" right through walls and ceilings. No wings. The tradition of angels with wings goes back to ancient times. Spiritual beings are usually surrounded by what observers call a glow or a light. This is nothing more exotic than the strong aura, which extends beyond human skin. With evolved beings, especially in the spiritual dimension, it can quite literally appear as a glowing envelope or cloak around the back and shoulders of the being.

The spiritual power we call "God" is universal, eternal, and positive. It never had an adversary or counter player, except what mankind has created for itself out of fear. Once we grasp this very simple truth, we are one step closer to leading positive, balanced lives.

Then which came first, the chicken or the egg? The spiritual universe surely created, or *manifested*, the physical universe. This view is based on the sequence between physical outer body and etheric, spiritual, inner body. Surely, the inner body came first and its physical counterpart followed. When the physical body is dissolved at death, the inner body continues right on to function in the spiritual dimension.

One of the great attractions of all religions is the hope that through it man can find a better life. Conversely, man frequently blames his failures to have a better life on a vengeful deity, on bad luck, on curses, on everything and anyone except himself. But it is precisely there where the blame must be placed.

How can a just God allow so much tragedy, so much suffering, and so much injustice in our world? If God is merciful, and He is, then why does he permit such conditions? These are complaints frequently heard, and the facts are there to support them. When man is faced with the inequities of life, he turns to prayer for help, to the Supreme Being who will fix things as a special favor. Man rarely examines his own conduct as a possible source of his problems.

This is definitely not the best of all possible worlds, but a world in great need of change and renewal to bring it back to its spiritual roots. Obviously, religion hasn't quite done the job. Progress in technology and inventions of a material kind have not changed the moral fiber of humanity one iota. There are things we can do on our own to change our life, and there are things we cannot change because they are due to what we may have done in a previous lifetime.

The evidence for reincarnation is overwhelming and I will not belabor this issue. Dr. Ian Stevenson of the Medical School at the University of Charlottesville, Virginia, the pioneer in this field, has written extensively about true cases of proven reincarnation. In my book *Life Beyond*, I have documented many cases where the recovered memory of a past existence cannot possibly be due to anything but genuine reincarnation. I have excluded the possibility of telepathic communications, of mediumistic communications from another personality, and still come up with significant numbers of case histories, both old and very recent, that cannot be explained in any other manner. Through years of research and experimentation, I have also found that mainly cases of lives that were abruptly terminated in one way or another lent themselves to exploration through hypnotherapy, and yielded tangible evidence. While we may all reincarnate, it is those whose lives ended in some unusual and often early fashion who are most likely to retain some memory of a previous existence.

The spiritual system demands a balance in a person's passage through a number of incarnations. That which was patently a wrong action in one life, must be balanced in the next. This is achieved by affording the person a chance to do better "this time around." Only by looking at our physical existence as the sum total of all our lives, can we understand the reasons for some seeming inequities and sufferings.

But we also have the opportunity to do something about them in this life. To begin with, understanding this concept and accepting it, helps change one's attitude from despair, anger, and resentment to one of hope: "What can I do to improve my situation in this lifetime?" We should realize that the spiritual system neither plays favorites, nor does it have a sentimental streak. It applies law to one and all equally and firmly, and it cannot be swayed by emotional outburst to make an exception.

The more obvious miseries in our lives are never in question. But there are other unhappy situations, in the broadest sense, which make our lives unhappy, that we simply take for granted and do nothing to change.

Illness and disease are still treated mainly by conventional medical standards, which concentrate on the physical body with little regard for the underlying etheric body where all illness really starts. Conventional medicine wants to make the sufferer feel better, even if it means suppressing the symptoms rather than attacking the cause. Fortunately, we now have some more open-minded physicians who take alternative medicine and its potential seriously.

Today all experiences and phenomena that seemingly defy the laws of ordinary science are being studied by properly qualified, academic people called parapsychologists. This does not include self-styled investigators whose sole credentials are their interest in the subject matter but have no really balanced training, which is so important in this field if it is to continue to be accepted as valid amongst the otherwise doubtful academic fraternity.

While Professor. Joseph B. Rhine started this new science, which is taken seriously in America, there have been other properly qualified researchers all over the world since the 19th-century German precursor of the field, Dr. Schrenk-Notzing. But it is also important to realize that the religion called Spiritualism, first very popular in England (and, later, in most of Europe) since the late 19th century, while *based* upon the evidence found by parapsychology, is not the same. The science is just that—a *science*—and must at times be cautious, whereas the religion is a matter of belief.

In my vocabulary, there are only three "dirty words" in this respect: *supernatural* (that is, without explanation), *belief*, and *disbelief*. Ultimately, the evidence, if carefully judged, must furnish the answer as to the nature of the phenomena.

Duke University, where Rhine first launched this science, was followed by other schools, such as the University of Virginia, in studying paranormal subjects, though without the power to offer a degree in this science.

Nothing, if properly presented with all the facts observed, is beyond an explanation, though not necessarily a commonly accepted one. In science, nothing stands still, and new opinions must be judged by their contents, not their newness.

PART ONE:

The Psychic

CHAPTER 1

PSYCHIC ABILITY: EXACTLY WHAT IS IT?

Michael was driving his car through the night, along a country road on which he had never been before. There was almost no traffic at that hour of the night. His mind kept wandering off to the performance he was to give the next day in a club far away from his home base. Suddenly, he saw another car, headlights blazing, coming toward him on the narrow road!

Michael looked again; there was no car. It was all in his head, he thought, as he resumed driving at full speed. But then he heard an inner voice repeatedly saying, "slow down, slow down." He did, and a moment later anther car was coming toward him, lights blazing—this time for real. Because Michael had slowed down, he was able to avoid hitting the other car and they passed each other, just barely. The incident shook him up, of course, but it hardly surprised him, because Michael had known for a long time that he had "the gift"...he was psychic.

June was hoping her application for that new, better job would lead to her getting the appointment. But she was far from sure. They said they would call her Wednesday, to let her know. Wednesday came, and June was nervously watching the telephone. The hours passed. Eventually she had to go out and run errands. She could not very well call her potential future employer to ask, do I get the job? She knew she had to wait for them to call her. But noon passed, and by 2:00 she knew she could wait no longer—she had to get to the market. She shrugged and went to the door. At that moment, a nagging hunch forced her to take her coat off and sit back down. Not more than a minute passed, then the telephone rang. Yes, she got the job. What made here delay her departure? June had realized, long before this incident, that she, too, was psychic.

The Psychic Sense

Do you know who is calling before the telephone rings? Do you dream of someone you haven't heard from in years, and they call the next day? Do you have a hunch you should avoid a certain flight, and it turns out they have engine trouble?

When you receive information about events in the future or occurring at a distance, and that information proves to be both accurate and totally unknown to you at the time you receive it, the explanation is most likely a talent usually referred to as *extrasensory perception* (ESP), or the psychic sense.

Scientists called parapsychologists have long established that ESP is not anything supernatural or to be feared. It is an integral part of human personality, albeit one that most of us have either ignored or neglected. Primitive people had it all along and used it, but as we became civilized and the environment in which we live became more crowded with distractions, that natural ability to pierce the veil of distance and time began to fade for most of us. Not, however, for everybody.

Being psychic is neither rare nor unnatural. If, for instance, you move into a house and you see someone who dissolves before your eyes, and it turns out that he or she used to live there but has died, you are not crazy—you are psychic.

What we used to call the "sixth sense" is really only the extension of our ordinary five senses stretched beyond what we used to think were their limitations, but in fact are not. The ability to stretch these senses varies among individuals, like any other talent or gift.

The psychic gift manifests in various ways. The most common form is simply foreknowledge of events in the future or from a distance. But some people also hear voices of the dead, or of the living from a distance—especially when there is urgent need to communicate because of crisis conditions—and others have seen apparitions, again both of the dead and sometimes the living, from a distance. These are projections—images—occurring for the purpose of contacting the psychic person, and in no way represent danger in and of themselves. Some religions hold that psychic phenomena, and the ability to perceive them, are undesirable, and conjure up colorful worlds of devils and demons; but the truth is, nothing is more natural and human than the psychic ability and its proper use.

Déjà Vu

Do you walk into a place and just know you've been there, and know what's in the next room—yet you never have been there before? Or perhaps you have had the sense that a particular event has actually happened before in your life. We call this *déjà vu*, which in the French language means "already seen." Many scientists attribute this phenomenon to what they call "temporal lobe misfiring," that is, a time delay in sensory images being received in the consciousness so that by the time one *does* become conscious of them, the image is already stored in the memory, giving the experiencer the impression that it was in his or her memory all along. But this is, at best, only a partial explanation—it can only address the most brief experiences of *déjà vu*, those only lasting a second or two. Many episodes last much longer, and to the parapsychologist these hint at reincarnation memories. This can be explored through regressive hypnosis, and if there is some unfinished business from another lifetime, it will come out.

Frances never left her native Georgia until her husband took her on their honeymoon trip to Florence, Italy. There she suddenly felt a compulsion to run ahead of her husband to an ancient palazzo, excitedly pointing out where the gate was and declaring the strong sense that she had lived there before.

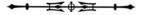

An American G. I. entered a farmhouse in Belgium during World War II and described to his buddies exactly and accurately what they would find at the top of the stairs—even though he had never been in that farmhouse before.

A Los Angeles housewife went to the Bavarian Inn at La Jolla, California, with her family for the first time, and could not take here eyes off the owner. Nor could he take his eyes off of her. They got to speak with each other, and they just knew they had met before! But he had just arrived from Germany, and she had never been to the Inn before in her life...well, that is in this life, at least.

These are just three of the countless similar stories I have heard during my years investigating the psychic. Déjà vu often indicates memories from past lives, a subject currently being studied seriously by leading parapsychologists. The evidence, consisting of detailed knowledge of previous lives that could not have been known to the person, is often compelling—though a vague feeling of having lived in Egypt or Tibet is hardly enough proof.

The psychic is all around us. At its lowest level it its instinct or intuition, maybe that inner voice that warns you of danger, or encourages you to make a move. It's a different order of things from the logical, rational world most of us trust—often far too much. It's a pipeline to the Beyond, and the Beyond is as real as this world.

We all have a gift for the psychic in varying degrees, just as anyone can learn to play the piano, but there is only one Paderewski, and only a few great pianists who make it to Carnegie Hall. Primitive man took that gift of second sight for granted: He needed it all right, to protect himself in a hostile, often uncharted environment. As modern man has developed his external technologies, the psychic gift has become relegated to the deepest levels of the unconscious. It is only natural that the less a thing is used, the more access to it dissipates. However, the trend can be reversed: The more you allow the psychic into your daily existence, and make it part of your consciousness, the more it will develop and benefit you. It is neither supernatural nor indicative of some sort of mysterious derangement if you know the so-called future, or things transpiring at a distance.

The science of Parapsychology has come a long way since its early days at Duke University in the late 1930s. But it has also left the lab and gotten into the mainstream of our daily lives.

Of course there is a great fascination with the ability to explore the future. Developing the ability, if there are some indications that you have that gift, is very simple: Accept it as natural, first of all, and use it whenever you can. You may touch an object belonging to a stranger and "see," with your inner eye, scenes from that person's past. This ability to receive impressions—whether visual or audible— via contact with an object in this way is called psychometry, and works because emotional events impress themselves on objects held by the person who experiences these events.

Getting the Most From a Psychic Reader

On matters concerning the future, however, the majority of people are more likely to consult a professional, because it may be assumed that a professional psychic reader has more of that gift than the average person.

At the most primitive end of the scale, it is the fortune-teller who is sought out when one needs advice about a problem besetting one at this moment, or because one is concerned about one's future. So-called Gypsy fortune-tellers are usually (but not always) con artists

who are best avoided, and they are not necessarily Gypsies either. You will find that reputable psychic readers seldom advertise with a sign for "Fortunes Told" in their window, and you will know them by their positive results recorded in consumer's guide books, such as my current *Hans Holzer's Psychic Yellow Pages*, as well as by any attention they have received in the media.

Don't let titles or terminology confuse you. Whether the person is called a psychic, a sensitive, a seer, or a medium, we are speaking about a similar gift, and these terms are largely interchangeable. One difference is that a medium is more likely to be the bearer of messages from the Other Side or to rely on a "helper" from over there.

If you feel the need to consult a professional psychic, there are certain safeguards to make sure you get your money's worth. In the first place, do not supply information concerning your question up front. Supplying such information will only serve to color or taint the reading, or to steer the reader. Do not ask specific questions about the specific people or situations you want answers for; just ask for a reading, and see what comes out. If the reader asks specific questions that you can answer only by supplying information about yourself, watch out. Ideally, you will sit there simply listening, while the psychic does all the talking. After the session ends, you can comment on it to the reader, if you wish to. But don't supply information on your own.

Can a psychic reader read your mind? No. But a psychic can scan your aura—the inner body we all have within us—where there is information about past and future events stored in a way a psychic may be able to tap into. This is something like a computer hard drive that has the data of your destiny written on it.

How does a reader get information? There is a vast array of techniques used by individual readers. Some may just sit opposite you and begin to speak. Some will see images; some will hear a voice or voices. Some may use a deck of cards or even a crystal ball, or touch an object worn by you, as described previously. Some may even do their work over the phone. But the information really comes from their own minds—or rather through the interface of your aura and their mind, not from any external tool.

The Trouble With 900 Numbers

Truly great psychics don't advertise; they don't have to. They are too busy. But there are professional psychics whose gift for self-promotion is as great as their gift for predicting the future. Making a decent living as a psychic is no more immoral than being a doctor or lawyer. But good doctors and lawyers don't send out brochures to mailing lists they purchase from professional advertising and promotion agencies, nor do they typically operate via 900 numbers while you pay by the minute for their advice.

In the last 10 years or so, an epidemic of telephone psychics has plagued the media. "Telephone psychics amaze callers with their powers," screams one ad (at $3.49 per minute). "Control your destiny—readings by LIVE psychics" (this one is $5 the first minute, $3 per minute thereafter—and they will keep you on the phone with double talk and banal generalities for as long as you, poor sucker, will allow it). There are dozens upon dozens of ads offering readings by "gifted psychics," "psychic discoveries network," "psychic experts for lovers and family," or "world-renowned psychics," and so on and so forth. In my opinion, these belong in the same category as those late and unlamented evangelical television ministries interested mainly in their followers' money. Last, but not least, a former Mrs. Sylvester Stallone, Brigitte Neilson, presents "the next level," through "the witches of Salem network" (at only $3.99 per minute). You can buy a lot of broomsticks with that, as long as the calls keep coming.

The psychics dispensing these telephone readings are neither genuine (though the law of average demands that once in a while a real psychic might just be among them) nor trained in any way.

So beware of the psychic 900 numbers. Lately such networks—usually fronted by a celebrity who has nothing whatever to do with the service—have done a landslide business. These so-called psychic networks, controlled by professional marketing people, use primarily inexperienced and untrained people to do readings. In my view these 900-number psychics are to be avoided even if, once in a while, a genuine psychic works for them because they need the money.

A further warning I would extend concerns a group calling itself the American Association of Professional Psychics, located in Baltimore, Maryland, and seemingly the brainchild of an astrologer and psychic (so she says) named Gail Summer. Now there is certainly need to sort out the false prophets from the real ones, but there is, of course, the matter of who does the testing, and who is really qualified to evaluate the results. I doubt very much that a self-styled association that tests would-be psychics by having them read for three of their board members is the answer. If the outfit likes the result of the tests, they will certify the would-be psychic as fit to enter the lucrative field of 900 numbers. There is a membership fee, of course.

However, whether this is a setup to connect with these questionable 900 services (the Baltimore group, according to their taped greeting to callers has links to the 900 business), or whether Ms. Summer really has her heart in the right place is, to me, a moot point. In my opinion, the troubling part is the qualifications of those testing the applicants and certifying them as bona fide readers.

By contrast to this group, I and other trained, professional researchers have, over the years, taken on the occasional gifted individual in search of training and testing. Only after long-term evaluation of results do we issue a letter certifying that the person involved has performed properly as a psychic reader or medium, as the case may be. And you may be sure there is no membership fee for our acknowledgement of their genuine gift.

No psychic can be 100 percent correct. Sometimes an event a psychic has predicted—or, more accurately, simply described—comes to pass exactly as foreseen. Sometimes it is a warning, and the client can avoid the event. Nothing is written in stone. You may receive a reading that implies a warning for you. In this case, you may use this information to change a present behavior or situation and thereby change the outcome.

ESP and Psychic Research

The traditional scientist will rightfully ask, how can anyone predict future events, in detail, before they have happened, sometimes even before the individuals involved have met? But people do, from Nostradamus, who foretold with great precision events both of an intimate nature between individuals and on a world scale before the principals had met, to many others, who were considered prophets throughout the ages. Some of our best contemporary professionals of the recent past, now passed over, such as Ethel Johnson Myers (with whom I did a lot of work involving hauntings), Betty Ritter, and the late Sybil Leek, did also. The greats, still living, such as Yolana Lassaw, Marisa Anderson, Carol Ann Appio, Peggy Esposito, Joy Herald, Judy Hoffman, Kathleen Carter, and Elizabeth Joyce, frequently—though not always—do, as well.

To accept this reality requires our rethinking of the nature of time and space, which Albert Einstein already questioned: Time is not an absolute, but a conventional dimension. Psychics can look outside the time stream and experience what lies ahead.

In the 1930s, when Duke University Professor J. B. Rhine dubbed psychic ability *extrasensory perception* (ESP), it was looked upon as a novelty. (Even into the early part of the 21st century, the link to anything spiritual or pointing toward the existence of a hereafter world has either been suppressed or gone largely unexamined.) The psychic talent was simply a natural component of human personality, an extension of man's psychological makeup that somehow could pierce the curtains of time and space. It took many more years of exploration before parapsychology, as the new science was called, would come up with the answers of its origin.

Because psychical research was satisfied to deal with laboratory tests, such as predicting a sequence of cards, or dice falling, and derive statistical information from them, the orthodox scientific community did not particularly object to the new science, seeing it employing familiar research patterns. It was only many years and thousands of recorded tests with hundreds of subjects later, that the futility of this method became clear. The observation and careful recording of actual phenomena, when they occurred, was now deemed more significant in the search for the origin of this mysterious gift.

In my own work, when I have taken on a gifted individual in search of testing that might verify psychic ability, the tests are many—ranging from psychometry tests, readings of strangers, visits to haunted locations (allegedly)—and may take several weeks. Extensive evaluation of results is necessary before certifying individuals' psychic abilities. In these affairs, it is a matter of importance who does the testing, and who is really qualified to evaluate the results. After more than 40 years in the field, I feel comfortable doing it.

In the last decades, communications technology has altered our image of the world we live in. What seemed like science fiction 20 years ago, is common place today. Dick Tracy's wrist telephone is a crude forerunner of our cellular telephones; wireless contact over huge distances in space is almost a routine in today's technological age. Jules Verne's Martian balloon may have amused the turn-of-the-century readership, but today we already know a lot about the Red Planet, because our instruments have already been there. Leonardo da Vinci actually designed a working submarine, but nobody took him seriously when even a steamship had not yet been invented.

And yet, mankind tends to respect inventions of the material kind, machines and devices that promise us a better life: You design it, you get the components, and you build it, and if you've done it right, it will work. But when it comes to unusual human faculties that transcend the limits of our knowledge of human ability at a particular time, mankind is very cautious. We can easily cope with transmissions by electronic gear over huge distances in space, because we understand how the gadget works. After all, we built it. But extrasensory perception, the psychic—where does it originate? Can we control it? Is it dangerous?

More and more, we study the effects of the psychic gift, and we try to deduce its system from these results. Only in recent years have serious professionals gotten into the work, parapsychologists who ignore the skepticism, even the outright hostility of their scientific brethren, in their efforts to understand and control the gift. Card and dice tests are rarely used these days, except for observation and experimentation, though the latter is not as fruitful in its results because clinical conditions tend to inhibit the performance of genuine psychics.

Opening Your Psychic Gift

The trouble with the psychic gift is that it does not conform to any of the rules and laws of empiric science. The phenomena cannot be duplicated at will in the laboratory. The psychic ability occurs randomly in people, and there is little evidence that it can be categorized, even though astrologers point to the preponderance of so-called "water signs" (those born under the astrological signs of Pisces, Cancer, and Scorpio) among people with unusual psychic ability.

We know a lot about the ordinary five senses, and the biochemical processes by which they function through our eyes, ears, tongue, olfactory system, skin, nerves, and so forth. But with the psychic sense, we know no such thing. Oh, there is that metaphysical talk about the Third Eye, and the various chakras or focal energy points of the body that are the basis of some alternative healing modalities, including acupuncture. But finding the actual organ, the seat of psychic power in man has thus far eluded us.

We cannot even be sure whether psychic ability is simply a function of the personality, differing in quality and intensity from person to person, or whether it is actually a channel, of sorts, through which other intelligences communicate information, which the psychic person then formulates into words, images, and sounds.

Regardless of its source or system, the psychic gift is a positive factor in us humans, because it immeasurably supplements our perception and ability to observe, even beyond what we usually perceive as the boundaries of time and distance.

A huge segment of the Earth's population has this gift, and it may well be that being psychic is the norm, while not having developed the gift is deprivation. It is patently not supernatural but perfectly natural, and there are ways to develop, enhance, and control it at will.

Whenever a person comes up with an answer that person would not normally possess, it has become common for someone to wonder out loud, "Are you psychic?" But it is not as simple as that. People can have shrewd guesses, informed opinions, be experts in a field, and, by the law of average, might just stumble upon the right answer. However, when the knowledge is specific and detailed, and the person has not had access to that information, psychic ability is most likely the source.

Every one of us is potentially psychic, just as every person normally endowed can see, hear, taste, feel, and smell. It is simply a matter of the degree. The psychic ability is the human birthright, and developing it depends greatly on your attitude toward it—reception or rejection—and usage of it. The more you let it happen, the more it will grow.

One simple way to test your own ability is to gather a group of people, maybe some friends, but also friends of friends—some people about whom you know nothing. Ask each one to hand you an object they carry on their person, like a key ring or a piece of jewelry (provided they are the only ones who have worn it). Take the item into your hand, relax, and say the first things that come to your mind.

They may be images, places, names, situations, whatever you feel like saying in a spontaneous, natural way. Ask that no one say anything until you are done, and especially not volunteer information about themselves. But when you are finished reading the object, ask them how accurate you have been. If you are reading for a group of friends—people whose history you know quite a bit about—try putting the objects into envelopes and mix them up so you do not know whom you are reading.

Keep score of your success and failures—your hits and misses—and don't be surprised that you experience a bit of both. If you find that you are about 50 percent accurate, you are certainly seriously psychic. Keep a log of statements concerning the future you make during these readings and check up with your subjects later to see how accurate your impressions turned out to be. If your psychic ability is primarily self-oriented, as in hunches and premonitions, by all means heed them without question.

There is inherently no difference between your having a natural psychic ability and a professional person making his or her living by using that power for the benefit of others, clients who pay for the service the way we pay doctors and lawyers for theirs. Whatever psychic ability you may have can manifest in a variety of ways. A hunch, an intuition, and a "funny" feeling about something or someone are all mild forms of psychic perception. On the other end of the scale is deep trance, the ability to go into a state of *dissociation of personality*, during which a personality seemingly different from your own speaks through and from you. These manifestations are comparatively rare and, in some instances, may be found to be an emotional or mental disturbance in an individual rather than an actual psychic trance. The proof may always be found in the nature of the information, the style of the communications, and other details, coming through an entranced person.

Just as some professionally trained mediums may have deep trance experiences, so might an ordinary individual, who is simply gifted with a raw, undeveloped psychic ability. However, by and large, psychic ability is the mental kind, that is, you are fully conscious while receiving these flashes of psychic insight.

Lastly, psychic ability comes to you naturally, if unsought, and in no way represents an evil force. Whether it is used for good or for exploitation (for selfish purposes) depends entirely on you. In all ages, all over the world, there have been large pockets of intolerance created by the extremist attitude of some religions. Foolish accusations are sometimes made by ignorant people as to the nature of the psychic, which they perceive to be "of the devil"—a personality existing only in their own feverish imagination, or employed as a power tool in the doctrines of hate religions. We need only remember that if we, our lives, are from God, so indeed is the psychic sense.

Foreknowledge of Danger

The sixth sense has been credited over and over with having saved people's lives by alerting them that danger to their person or to a loved one was just around the corner. Many, for instance, have received a warning not to take a certain airplane. Or to avoid a certain street at night, because it was unsafe. But sometimes, rather than a warning, we receive a simple *knowing* that all will not be well. While not pleasant, this can still be considered helpful because it may allow us to be more ready for bad news with which we will, in any case, have to cope.

> *Mrs. J. B. could not sleep all night because she just knew something was wrong with her son. Sure enough, the next morning there was that call informing her that he had suffered an accident.*

◆—◆ ▰◆▰ ◆—◆

> *Ben R. was unusually emotional when he said a casual good-bye to his old friend from college days, Louis, because in his heart of hearts he knew he would never see his friend again. Sure enough, a week later, the friend passed away.*

The Inner Voice

People claiming to hear voices are usually considered psychotic in one way or another: Multiple personality is still considered by most psychiatrists a form of split personality to be treated as such and not—perhaps—possession, although I know for a fact that, in such cases, possession is always a possibility.

But here we are talking about something else. As for myself, I am constantly hearing voices: the voice on the radio, on television, the voice of my daughter talking on the telephone in the next room, the voice of my agent telling me to be patient, the voice of the lady from out of town on the bus who wants everybody to hear her life story. But the voice I like to hear most of all is the inner voice, because it is my direct link to the truth. We all have it—that odd feeling about things, events, and people that is beyond reason.

When I was 18, I naturally knew all the answers. I just did not know all the questions. That came later—more questions than I ever thought existed, about the future, about my abilities to succeed, about my friends and loves. I am no longer 18, and I know there is no end to questions, especially the unanswered kind. But we do get a chance to sort them out and address them. Addressing an unanswered question is a lot like addressing a letter and mailing it. You are not quite sure if it will ever get to its destination, but you sure hope so.

As the years went by, I learned a lot about the world, and I dealt with the world's matters as most people would: rationally, sensibly, and as reasonably as possible, allowing for my temper. I never considered myself normal or average, but I knew I lived in what passes for a normal world, and if I were to succeed in it, I needed to deal with it in terms that the world understood and was likely to accept. I did not go to a meeting with a banker (hoping for a motion picture loan) wearing sports clothes and a crystal on a chain. I wore a blue suit and a tie—an appropriate costume, the way you wear white shorts on the tennis court.

But, although I always knew how to fit in with mainstream expectations, there was always a force residing within me (and, I am sure, within all of us) that would not conform to the outer reality I lived in. Early on in my life, I felt the need to come to terms with that force: I could either ignore it or allow it to counsel me, and I chose the latter.

That force, which I came to call my inner voice, was always on my side, never against me. Sometimes it told me things I did not want to hear at the time, but in retrospect, I always wished I had listened—always.

It could be upsetting, perhaps even frightening to acknowledge the existence within myself, of so powerful and omniscient a force, but once I realized that the inner voice derived its knowledge not from me but from some other, larger external pool of understanding, I was at peace. And I saw myself as the recipient of a favor.

For instance, I would be writing a book, and turn in the manuscript to my editor. Instantly I knew how he would react, and sure enough he did what my inner voice told me he would do. At first, I let things happen, without trying to take advantage of the inner voice. Gradually, I came to trust the voice more and more. If my nudge told me, the editor was not going to like it, I took another look at the book and made changes, until the nudge turned positive and confident.

I can deal with problems and challenges in two ways: through analysis (which includes logic and reasoning) or by turning to my inner voice for counsel—counsel that can take various nonverbal forms, all the way from a simple nudge to a full-fledged premonition. The equality of the sexes not withstanding, it is a fact that the majority of men tend to follow the first path, and most women, the second. These two paths are incompatible by their very nature, we are often told, forcing us to make a choice as to which to follow. But I have discovered a third approach, which combines the best of the other two.

The way of reason and the way of intuition differ in many important aspects. Reason is sharply defined (even if it turns out to be wrong) and intuition is generally vague. There are some things we can do, as individuals, to improve these faculties. Weighing all possibilities and alternatives before arriving at a reasonable conclusion gives me a sense of confidence for having done all I can do to define the problem and its possible solution. Relaxing the inner self, so it becomes more conducive to receiving those impulses and feelings associated with the intuitive process, helps deepen it and make it a bit more precise. (Means of accomplishing the latter may differ from person to person—for some it may be yoga, for others, meditations, for others still, simply taking a walk can be effective.)

Curiously, reason is always of the moment, and takes into account only that which is now, and what went on up to this moment. The future is speculative at best. But intuition, represented by the inner voice, knows no such boundaries of time and space. It extends with equal force into the so-called future as it does with the present, and the past is of no interest to it at all. Clearly, if the inner voice can tell me accurately what I should do or what I may expect, our conventional concepts of time and space need some revisions.

Reason, employing chiefly the thought process associated with the brain as a kind of human switchboard, is also limited by the very nature of that process. Intuition (and its instrument, the inner voice) partakes of feelings, which would seem to originate elsewhere in the human personality—whether the traditional heart of the poet, or the more realistic solar plexus of the spiritually oriented—is a moot question. In this age of consciousness expansion (and the rediscovery of some very old truths about our nature), being able to combine the best of both these worlds is naturally desirable.

To combine the strengths of both paths, whatever the situation, problem, question, or decision to make—whether on a social plane or business—do what the investment community does when it is asked to deal with a new project. Exercise due diligence, the careful, measured investigation of the people involved from whatever sources are available—business associates, references, friends. That provides the external picture. Now one can turn to the intuitive channel for the internal read, and the inner voice makes the final decision.

If one disregards the reason part of this process, then there might be lingering doubt about the validity of the inner voice, which would tend to diminish its powers. Also, by embarking first on the conventional road, more input is obtained and fed into the human computer, making the inner voice that much more effective and knowledgeable.

> *A friend of mine met a man with a fine talent for selling real estate. He so much liked the fellow he was ready to plunge. "I just got this feeling about the guy," he would tell me, "I knew this was an opportunity I couldn't pass up." Well, in the end, he did have to give his due diligence, and that was when he learned an unsavory truth about his man. As soon as he had digested it, his inner voice finally told him to lay off the deal, and this time, he listened.*

Why didn't his inner voice warn him off to begin with? Because he let his personal judgment guide him, based not on true intuition but an observation, and observation is only first cousin to analysis and reasoning!

Men nearly always prefer the rational approach to their problems: If it fails, they are not ashamed; they have done their best. But if a man uses intuition to deal with his problems instead of reason, and still fails (perhaps because he did not quite understand the gentle nudges his inner voice was giving him) he will be angry with himself, and feel foolish for having used this path.

Not so with the ladies: Women have always been able to accept the gift of intuition as perfectly natural, by and large. The physical differences between the sexes are matched by emotional differences, at least generally speaking. The question is, why are women more likely to welcome and utilize that element of intuition in their personalities that I have come to call the inner voice?

> *"I did not like Fred the moment I met him," confided my friend Kim, who is 35, gorgeous, and unattached, "though common sense told me he was attractive, well-mannered, had an important position in the business world, and came on to me like a blockbuster." But the inner voice told Kim to consider him with due diligence. It turns out that he was very much married, in another city.*

Whenever the inner voice warns against a partner, prospective or already actual, it is wise not to disregard it, because the inner voice gets its information far ahead of our conscious mind. It is a little like a personal CIA—secretive, tyrannical, but always concerned with the well-being of its host.

Going against the expected, the most likely scenario, does not come easy for most people. "What is the point of telephoning this guy at 10:00 at night at his office to see about our deal?" I asked myself, having heard my inner voice urging me to do just that. And then I dialed. Sure enough, someone picked up, and we talked about our deal for half an hour . . . enough to close the following week.

Where does the inner voice get its information? If you are indeed psychic, it may well be a communication from a discarnate personality outside yourself. But if the voice is actually soundless, not really a voice actually heard, then it is most likely a deeper level of your own consciousness speaking up, reaching conscious level, and there is no outside voice involved. In the final analysis, it matters little whether accurate information derives from self at a deep emotional level that can somehow penetrate the now, to look ahead into the so-called future, whether some as yet little understood human faculty, such as extrasensory perception, makes this possible, or whether a friendly spirit guide whispers into one's inner ear. If it works, use it.

Apart from letting this force express itself freely, without trying to stifle or edit it, physical contact with another person also can be helpful for giving the inner voice a boost. Shaking hands, a kiss, and a simple touch all are conduits from one person to the other, which the intuitive apparatus analyzes immediately and feeds back to the conscious mind as a hunch, nudge, warning, or whatever is appropriate.

By making the inner voice a natural, functioning element of one's personality, dependence on outside support is diminished. Truly, how can a good friend, no matter how close; or a kindly minister, rabbi, or priest; or even a "shrink," no matter how well trained and intended, know more about what is good for us than one's own, unique, unbiased inner voice?

The Curious Importance of Age

As I've mentioned, women tend to listen to their intuitive nudges more often than men. So why is it that my young daughter listens to what her friends say, but my late grandmother would not even discuss the inner voice?

Why is it that women tend to have better intuition and listen more often to their inner voice, at certain times in their lives? Interestingly, it has been my observation that the majority of extraordinary examples of premonitions and other hunches, which actually come true, occur among women between the ages of 18 and 50, which also happens to be the most active period of their romantic, emotional, and sexual lives.

Over the years, I have worked with several dozen women who came to me for advice regarding their gift. To some, it was a frightening and unwanted addition to their personality, and they wanted me to permanently close their "psychic door," which I did, reluctantly, through hypnotherapy. I say reluctantly, because the gift of the inner voice is not a freak addition to personality, but a natural, primeval part of human emotion. To lack that voice is regrettable. To suppress or ignore it is even more so. Other women wanted their exciting gift enhanced, explored, and perhaps used in some practical way. I explained that acceptance of its existence and respect for its counsel would automatically enhance it. A few wanted to become professional sensitives; with these, I agreed to monitor their predictions and their scores.

Looking back now over the past more than 30 years as a researcher and writer, I find that age 23 is particularly common as a time when this expanded consciousness called the inner voice manifests strongly for the first time. It also seems to get stronger after 40, and typically begins to decline after 60 years of age, though this is not always the case.

Psychic Tools and "Toys"

At times, a legitimate psychic will make use of various accessories, perhaps to tune her reception, so to speak. In other instances, these tools are used by a spirit in order to communicate directly when, perhaps, the questioner's skill is not matched by his or her desire to make contact. I wish to make it clear from the outset, that I do not feel all such extraneous "helpers" are to be condemned or ignored. But I must question some of the usage to which they are put in many instances.

Ouija Boards

Also called the *planchette*, Ouija boards were introduced post World War I, used by the grieving who hoped to hear from lost loved ones now in the spirit world. The board is imprinted with the letters of the alphabet, numbers, and, oftentimes, the words *yes* and *no*, which allow a cursor (ostensibly controlled by a spirit on the Other Side, though the questioner's fingers rested atop it), letter by letter, to form the replies to questions raised by the seeker.

When such attempts are successful and a contact does result that cannot be explained by the questioner's own knowledge of the person whose contact is sought, the result is still not due to the tool itself—a piece of wood or plastic—but to the psychic ability of the querant and/or contact. The same result might be obtained by a psychically attuned individual just sitting quietly and opening him- or herself to the inner voice.

Ouija boards, in fact, are potentially dangerous as contact devices if the one making the contact is a negative or disturbed spirit. A case with which I am very familiar involved a lady who whiled away the time with a Ouija board while on vacation with two companions. She fell victim to an entity gaining entrance to her through this device, and the sad result was that she could not get rid of that entity who had been a criminal in his physical life. After she resumed drinking, despite my advice to avoid such weakening habits, she became totally unable to shake the entity. Even the professional work of three people—a trance medium, the head of psychiatry at a big hospital (who was also a parapsychologist), and I—could ultimately not help her. She ended up totally psychotic.

Young people and children, particularly those who might have seen the Ouija board advertised as a harmless toy, had best stay away from it. It does not offer a better contact than meditation by a psychic person, and it can be harmful.

Crystal Balls

Crystals are concentration objects to allow the psychic person to focus in on messages coming through. By themselves, they have no power whatever but, when used by a psychic person, can focus his or her psychic abilities considerably. Even so, any information gained via the use of a crystal ball is information the  psychic would have been able to obtain by other means: The object itself yields nothing new or extra.

Cards

Cards, on the other hand, can be very useful if the one using them is strongly psychic, because the cards are interpreted according to what the reader's psychic sense suggests, not by what a guidebook or such offers as explanation for the reading of the tarot cards. Ordinary playing cards do not offer such potential interpretations, only real tarot will be useful, no matter what the individual designs are.

Pendulums

The pendulum—a suspended weight of metal or crystal—is generally able to answer only with yes or no, and as such is not very useful in questions that require some detail or other kinds of information. Because it is held by hand, one must also seek the source of its wisdom: in the unconscious of the person holding it, and not in the pendulum itself.

In conclusion, the weight of evidence shows that the power of receiving (and sending) psychic information rests with the person doing it and not with any man-made object. There also are a number of machines and devices promising all kinds of improvements of one's mental ability, and they should be avoided. Psychic ability is a natural gift that comes with the person—not with any artificial device.

CHAPTER 2
THE PSYCHIC NATURE OF ANIMALS

There is hardly a pet owner who does not claim his pet fully understands him, and vice versa. Domestic pets are not simply animals. They are part of the household, part of a human being's life. It is tempting to ascribe this special relationship to the pet's human environment, even to the influence of the boss. But that is merely one element, and a surface one at that.

Long before contemporary people went to the pound or the pet store to pick out a particularly attractive dog, adopted an orphaned kitty, or bring home a bird in a cage for company, the animal factor in the life of human beings—the spiritual linking of humankind and the beasts—was fully understood and considered perfectly normal in cultures going back thousands of years and all over the globe. Only the so-called Age of Reason, initiated by the unfortunate French Revolution, did away with all such "superstitions" and attempted to separate the human species from the Animal kingdom.

It is too bad those revolutionary French had not viewed the cave paintings at Lascaux! Early primitive man admired the strength and cunning of animals and sometimes dressed in their skins to assimilate the animal's powers into himself. That was their belief, and the belief of their enemies, too. In one example, this might result in a warrior painted as a Mayan tiger, or jaguar, engaged in battle with a sly, masked monkey. We have ample testimony for the blending of animal features with human characteristics in the pantheons of Egyptian gods,

47

even Greek heroes (or demigods), and the belief, not yet so dead, of werewolves and vampires (both of which will be seen to in Chapter 10). Here we are dealing with two types of animal beings: gods, capable of intervening in human affairs, in the shape of an animal, and gods in human form, with animal parts, functioning fully as deities.

Sahkmet, the cat, is Egypt's goddess of war. As her appearance is no different than any ordinary cat, if you had run into her in the streets of ancient Memphis or Thebes, you really would not know whether to pet her or worship her—unless of course she talked to you first! Another cat goddess is the domestically inclined Bast, the ever-watchful moon goddess. Similar in some ways to Bast, but appealing more to "dog people" perhaps, were the Chinese "temple dogs" of the Far East, considered animal-bodied guardians of the household. Actually, they are not dogs at all, but Chindvits, or magical lions. However, to the casual observer, they do look a bit like Pekinese!

Anubis, one of the lesser gods of Egypt, is a man with the head and neck of a jackal, not because the combination looks interesting, but because the jackal's qualities, added to man's abilities, make him a god. The sphinx, with the body of a lioness, a bird's wings (in some cases), and a woman's face needs scarcely to be explained— it is a powerful combination in any culture, and the sphinx, a notorious keeper of secrets and poser of riddles,  is a part of the religious life of ancient Greece, pre-Columbian America, and even the mythos of Celts and Baltic people.

A close cousin to the various sphinxes is the griffin, believed to be resultant of a lion and an eagle mating. Like the sphinx, they purportedly drew their power from the sun, and today survive as heraldic  animals, their image emblazoned on family armor, symbolizing vigilance. The heraldic use of an animal's image both proclaimed qualities a given family purported already to possess, and called upon those qualities for protection. In earlier times, people feared dragons and their smaller chimerical brethren, the griffins, although certainly nobody has ever seen either one!

Cerberus, a three-headed dog, was believed by the Greeks to guard the gates of the Underworld, and both griffins and dragons were thought to stand guard of certain places they considered their territory. In the Middle Ages, certain mountains or rivers were "ruled" by a dragon, and one had better stay away from that place. Even as late as the 16th century, people believed that at the bottom of certain deep wells there lived a monster called the Basilisk. Not your average pet in appearance, the Basilisk was in the well because that was his well, and he did not wish people to use it. Even nonexistent animals have been given only too human qualities, such as greed and possessiveness.

Of course some animal characteristics in otherwise human-looking deities are not necessarily spiritual, but practical. Pan, the Greek deity of pastures, flocks, and herds, had a goat's feet and legs because the goat was the principal animal of ancient Greek farmers. His appearance made this agricultural god familiar to his worshippers. The Celtic hunting god Cernaunos wore a stag's crown, not because it gave him the reasoning power of the stag (not all that great), but, to the contrary, to attract the unsuspecting stag and provide food for his people as a result.

Birds—both wild and tame—have also, at times, had strange powers attributed to them far beyond a bird's capabilities. The hawks who had followed the rise and fall of the Imperial Habsburgs, a family that ruled in Europe for centuries, were supposed to take off for good, once the Habsburgs were finished. They sure did, in 1918, as soon as the Central Powers sued for peace, and the Habsburgs abdicated, and went into permanent exile (but this is a story for Chapter 11).

Edgar Allan Poe's celebrated poem, "The Raven," equates the black bird with destiny and an omen, and some ravens can indeed be trained to imitate human speech. Do they also understand it?

A Native American shaman might use a bird in certain ceremonies, or even shape-change to become one himself, in order to perform an act anonymously or to travel far and fast. In Wicca, the "craft of the wise" (commonly called witchcraft), a modern adaptation of ancient Earth religions, the *familiar*, or messenger, is the black cat. Historically, such beliefs led to persecutions, accusations of devil worship (which witches don't do), and many poor cats were slaughtered in the Middle Ages right into the "enlightened" 18th century—

victims of man's ignorance. The familiar is not an evildoer, but the witch's go-between to perform magic, or to help people in trouble or who are ill. Why a black cat? Because cats move quietly, and the color black makes them invisible in the night when Wiccans perform their rituals.

When we combine animal traits and graft them onto human bodies, we are dealing with imaginary creatures whose impact on people is religious and spiritual. But when we consider regular animals, even pets, to have special powers or missions, we are imbuing the Animal kingdom with the possibility of transcending the usual and accepted limitations of their world and intelligence.

Odysseus' faithful dog, who alone recognized his master on his return from a long journey, is clearly not your average pet. Dogs in particular have played important and special roles in the Catholic church, from which we get St. Rochus, patron saint of dogs. Faithful—that is, abiding, full of faith—is the criterion here, something you can sometimes expect from the human species, but not really from "dumb" animals.

In spiritual symbolism, Judeo-Christian religions of contemporary times are little different from the pantheistic bestiaries of antiquity. The Holy Spirit is usually shown as a white dove, not a person or a bright light, as one might expect. A dove is sent forth by Noah to explore the land and returns with an olive branch. The symbiosis between man and animal runs deep, although perhaps some of it has been lost in an age of relentless industrialization and materialistic thinking.

Holy men still commune with animals without difficulty—but on what level? Surely, it is not on the intellectual level but rather on the spiritual level, which truly runs from man to animal to plant without interruption. To paraphrase Einstein, who stated that on "the subatomic level time and space are interchangeable," on the spiritual level, all beings are equal. (The line between human beings and the animal world also disappears in the East Indian belief in transmigration—the reincarnation of a human soul into an animal and vice versa. The belief is based on the need for man to rise from the lower forms to the top, if humankind can be referred to as so exalted. However, while there is plenty of scientific proof of human reincarnation, there is none for transmigration.)

But now what are we to make of such anomalies as Jeff, the talking mongoose, a celebrated English case of the paranormal, or the talking horse who can add and multiply? Both are actually pronouncing words in human language—clearly, not a possible talent of these creatures.

There we deal, I am convinced, with rare incidents of animal mediumship, where animals, pets, serve as communicators between a discarnate person and the physical world. Far fetched? Not really, when one considers that the mechanics of mediumship are exactly the same as between people.

Lastly, we do have a category of "literary animals," who are animals, especially pets, in body only, who speak good English and converse with people or other animals, as brightly as people do, or sometimes even more so.

Alice's companions, from the March hare to the dormouse, have all the foibles of humans, and are of course a device to present satirical commentary upon contemporary society, in this case the stuffy Victorian World.

Hugh Lofting, a veterinarian by trade, is immortal through his fictional *Dr. Dolittle* who lives with, speaks with, and even travels with all sorts of animals—pets and others—all of whom have their own distinct personalities and views.

Do the children who read such books really believe they can have a talking dog or cat or bird? Probably not. By and large, children are not stupid. Still they love the fantasy, and they understand very well that while human speech may be less than possible for their favorite pets, they are definitely capable of more than a simple meow or bark.

Disney's cartoon animals are so enjoyable to young and old because we recognize, in their behavior, our own good selves. Bambi, for example, is fictional, yet this cartoon fawn's image did more for humans' care for deer than any scientific report full of statistics could have done. We desperately want our animals—wild animals and pets alike—to talk to us, partake in our human lives.

How much reality is there in a jungle hierarchy that recognizes the lion as King? In actual fact, it is the qualities of the lion that we recognize as majestic. To "humanize" animals in our stories, even as the ancients did, is conducive to reminding us how much we share with our animal companions, and that animals are God's creatures too.

When a beloved pet dies, the bond between pet and master does not just evaporate. Far from it, cases of animals continuing to be seen, heard, or felt by their families long after they have died, are not uncommon. Even ghosts of wild animals or of farm animals have been reported, but it is the peculiar human bond that seems to make spirit pets more numerous among reports of this kind.

Pauline is a professional spiritualist whom people seek out for sittings in her native Manchester, England. "There are often animals when I have private sittings," she explained, "they have lived with my sitters and come along and sometimes just sit by them. I asked one lady, did she know a white cat I saw in spirit, and she instantly identified her as her late pet."

Mrs. Audrey L. of Canada actually saw the soul leave the body of her beloved cat, Ginger. "I was with him when he died and a small light left his body and floated up the stairs to a person holding out his hands for Ginger. I have often wondered if it was my husband or my father. Then the cat settled on his lap."

Mrs. C. D. of California had an extremely smart cat who was killed on the highway, though she did not know this at the time it happened. At first, she assumed the cat had run off or been lost, but the second night after the cat's disappearance, she saw her in a vivid dream and got the message, somehow, that her pet had died. Sure enough, a day later she found out the truth.

John D. of Oklahoma tells me of a family dog he had by the name of Blackey. The dog had appointed herself the watchdog, and every night she would go from room to room, kitchen to living room, down the hall, and finally back to her mat at his parents' bedroom. But as the dog grew old, she was no longer so surefooted, and finally she ran into a little table, which fell over with a crashing sound. A few days later, her illness forced the family to put the dog "to sleep," as they say. But that was not the end of Blackey. Far from it. So used to making the rounds of the house, night after night, she continued to do so, albeit unseen by the family. A few nights after her passing, the sound of Blackey was plainly audible as she still "made the rounds," including the crash of the table falling over. This continued for a while until John D. said a prayer for her release, and all has been quiet ever since.

Katherine R. of San Francisco, a very psychic lady, was living in Eugene, Oregon, when her pet cat Sam got run over by a car and died underneath their porch. For a long time after she would hear the cat's peculiar crying in that spot, and see the cat herself out of the corner of her eye while watching TV. Another cat named Ichabod, who was also unfortunately killed by a car, would come into the living room, sit in front of the television, wag his tail, and then slowly disappear.

Miss H. E. of New Jersey had to put their 18-year-old dog named Lady Dog "to sleep" but felt terribly guilty about it, despite the fact that the dog was truly ill. But at night, when Miss H. E. was reading in bed, she often would feel the weight of her pet on bed, and when she touched the cover, it was warm, as if a living animal had lain on it.

She began to say prayers at the spot where the dog used to sleep and sometimes she would see what she described as "a tiny white spot, like a tiny light" and felt a presence in the room.

Mrs. Robert W. of Indiana had a little dog named Sugar who took sick and, at almost 11 years old, died rather unexpectedly, though the veterinarian had assured her that the dog was fine. The W.'s had no children and were very close to their pet. About four months later, they were talking about how much they missed the little dog, *when both clearly heard a long, pitiful moan from the direction of where their dog had slept. The bed had been left untouched in their bedroom.*

About a month after that, Mrs. W. heard Sugar's bark; there was no mistaking it. It reassured her that life went on beyond death, even for little dogs.

Even living pets may have problems with ghost pets, just as people sometimes have with ghosts. Take the case of a Siamese named Sam:

Sam used to live with Mrs. Ann F. M. of North Carolina. Poor Sam was hit by a car and departed this world, and Mrs. F. got another cat to take his place. Or rather, this was her intention. However, five days after Sam's death, his voice came from what was apparently an empty room, where he had slept when still in the body. The other cat, Spooky, did not like sharing the room with a spirit cat— obviously she was hearing the voice of her predecessor— and as a result, her personality changed. In the end, Mrs. F. decided she could not handle both cats and opened the front door to let the live cat go, which she did with great dispatch. After that, the spirit cat never made any noise again. No need to, she had prevailed.

Undoubtedly, there must be tales of spirit birds and other animals people like to keep, but cats and dogs are the favorites. Could it be that they are more apt to be psychic in physical life, and therefore able to continue the bond with us? Perhaps one of the most astounding (and yet perfectly natural) accounts of the interplay between people and spirit animals comes from Mrs. Gertrude O. in Canada:

"For 17 years we had a beautiful Persian cat who seemed at times almost human. Eventually he died of old age as I held him in my arms.

"About three days after his death, I was lying in bed when I felt what seemed like a cat walking around in the vicinity of my feet. He was purring at quite a rate—I could feel the vibrations of his purring."

Apparently, the same thing also happened to Mrs. O.'s daughter. The cat has been around them ever since.

"I have become so used to having him sleeping on my bed that I miss him when he does not come. His habits are just the same as when he was alive. He always took turns sleeping on my or my daughter's bed, usually spent a month in each room, and he still does the same things. I have seen him come through the wall between her room and mine and walk slowly down the bed, his eyes shining like jewels . . . he emits a bluish light . . . from which shoot little star-like sparks. When he descends on the bed, sometimes one has the sensation that he is resting on a skin or balloon like substance. . . . "

Evidently, animals inhabit a spirit "body" just as humans do when they first pass over to the Other Side.

CHAPTER 3

PREDICTING THE FUTURE: FROM CLAIRVOYANCE TO PROPHECY

Since time immemorial, people have consulted professional psychics for personal reasons, usually having to do with health, wealth, and love. We are living in a period when interest in the psychic is greater than ever before, perhaps because we now live in a world filled with violence and uncertainties. However, these days, we are also accustomed to scientific verification and less given to accepting the psychic as the "magic" it once appeared to be. We want our psychics scientifically certified, so to speak. I have personally investigated many psychics and worked with some very fine trance mediums as well, and I have also learned that there are those who are excellent, average, and some who are really no good at all.

Today the professional trance medium, working primarily with the likes of me, are not fortune-tellers for anxious individuals. In a recent directory called *Hans Holzer's Psychic Yellow Pages* you can find them all listed with details of past work and records. For the person wanting to know about their own, individual future, a so-called psychic reader is the best possibility, not a deep trance medium, though in some instances a session with a deep trance medium may yield a direct contact with someone on the Other Side of Life, a relative or friend whom the sitter (you) would recognize.

Channeling, Past Lives Readings, and the Occasional "Star Person"

Now and then, a 900-number psychic will quote a channeling source speaking through them, dispensing counsel to the client. Genuine psychics own up to what they tell their clients. They do not defer to a nebulous channeling personality as their source. Good psychic readers give specifics, not pseudo-pastoral council—not what the client most likely wants to hear.

But then we come to a group of guileless, self-proclaimed, metaphysical individuals, usually coming from pretty ordinary and even dull lives, who somehow discover their uniqueness and wish to share it with the masses of believers. More often than not, they profess coming "from the stars" and not being really like the rest of us earthlings.

Solara Antara Amaa (they also create exotic sounding names) is big in cosmic consciousness, teaching her own brand of New Age philosophy. Unlike the 900-number vultures, she (and others of her ilk) does no great harm, in my opinion, nor does she offer anything more than a philosophy of her own making. Those interested in this sort of thing can contact her organization:

Star-Borne Unlimited
2005 Commonwealth Drive
Charlottesville, VA 22901
Tel: (804) 293-1111

Closely related to channeling is the proliferation of so-called past-lives readings. In the latter, a psychic will tell a client right off the bat who the client was in previous lives. Whether the information given includes actual names and places or not, usually, the details of such earlier lifetimes are incapable of being checked out scientifically, rendering such information fairly useless.

My objection with such practices is that they obscure the very real and highly important research into reincarnation and genuine evidence for prior lives that has indeed been obtained. (At the University of Virginia's Department of Psychiatry, for instance, Dr. Ian Stevenson founded an investigation unit expressly for the study of reincarnation; he is succeeded in his work there by Dr. James Tucker) I will be talking much more about the phenomenon of channeling in Chapter 6.

Prophecy

When it comes to the future of our world, people tend to fall into roughly three categories. First are those who really don't believe in any kind of prophecy or psychic predictions. Second are those who are totally convinced that the predictions of the great prophets—from St. John to Nostradamus, from Malachy to Edgar Cayce—will come to pass exactly as made, and who live in a kind of undercurrent of fear of it all. Finally, the third are those who are impressed by the track record of prophecies fulfilled, and try to balance the likely with the unlikely by examining the track record of past prophecies.

I belong to the latter group, and thanks to my training and long experience as a professional parapsychologist, can look at the prophecies dispassionately and rationally, more so as I consider it my task to sort it all out for the large masses of people who really aren't sure, and wish they were. Over the years, I have learned, from empiric evidence studied carefully from many sources, that there is no such thing as 100 percent accuracy among those who would predict the future. On the other hand, one can blame that on the lack of human perfection, because, after all, psychics, mediums, and prophets are people, and the information they give us must be filtered through their personalities and minds.

On the other hand, could it not be the *intent* of the system, whatever you wish to call that system, or law, or Divine Providence, to let us have just so much certainty and no more, and to give us foreknowledge only when it is proper for us to have it? I think so. It is a system that will at once help humanity along by hinting at what is yet to come, and still encourage our dealing with it, preparing for it, and to choose the right path, based on what bits and pieces of advance knowledge we are given. We can call this *destiny, karma,* or *free will*—take your pick. It is still a very orderly and, I think, fair system: We cannot possibly earn good karma if we are not making decisions and choices, taking actions—the system provides us with opportunities, with encounters carefully programmed ahead of our becoming aware of them in the time stream, but the system also expects us to be individuals and express our preferences.

As I see it, yes, there is for each of us a destiny up ahead, and we are not immune to its powers. But destiny has its rules and laws, and within those we have a great deal of freedom of choice. How we choose will depend primarily on who we are, that is, what our personality is like in this lifetime, and how we use our gifts, abilities, talents, sense of judgment, sense of fairness, and understanding of what is patently evil and what is obviously good.

Thus, while prophets can and do predict the coming of catastrophes of one kind or another, they cannot always predict the effect it may have on an individual when the event strikes, and there is, in addition, a certain margin for error, in that we have the power to deflect the event once we understand its likelihood, and counteract its oncoming influence in ways that would balance any negative force with the power of the positive, both individually, and as part of groups and movements.

Prophecies can be of two kinds: events foretold that will surely occur, and events that may occur but are still subject to being changed, if certain steps are taken by mankind. It is unfortunately not always clear with which kind of prophecy we deal, but sometimes it is, especially when determined people refuse to accept the inevitable and fight back in whichever way they know how, to alter the outcome of the dire prophecy. Then the prophecy becomes a warning prophecy, something parapsychology calls a *premonition*.

Nostradamus

No documented prophet in relatively recent times has been as detailed, accurate, and of course, upsetting to humanity because of the nature of some of his prophecies, than Michael Nostradamus, a 16th-century French physician and astrologer. Dozens of books have been written about his prophecies, with all kinds of interpretations and translations, many of which are either false or misunderstood. There is also one book by the late Henry Roberts, a New York antiquarian book dealer, who had become so obsessed with his Nostradamus studies, that eventually he became convinced that he was, in fact, Nostradamus reincarnated. Alas, among the many books giving Nostradamus's prophecies, Mr. Roberts's is least likely to be reliable.

As a matter of fact, the most accurate of all Nostradamus scholars was the late Stuart Robb, who passed on just recently, a man whom I knew well, and who was not only a leading scientific investigator of the paranormal, but also a great musicologist and authority on the classic composers, such as Richard Wagner, whose works he translated.

I am very confident with Robb's translations and interpretations of the quatrains, or verses, which Nostradamus used to camouflage his prophecies. Such camouflage was necessary because in his time, enlightened renaissance though it was, it still was not healthy to prophecy the murder of a king of the country in which one lived, or the destruction of the papacy in centuries to come. In Spain particularly, but also elsewhere in Catholic Europe, the Inquisition was rampaging and burning anyone daring to have ideas about the future, because clairvoyance was considered witchcraft, and witches were to be destroyed for being in league with the devil—the same devil so carefully constructed by a special committee of the church under orders from Pope Innocent III, assigned to find a worthy opponent to Christian theology. By accusing dissenters of worshipping this figment of the church's imagination, it was possible to do away with the opposition. Those sophisticated enough to read between the quatrains' lines or understand the hints he gave in the verses, had no great trouble understanding, though some of the hints still are controversial today.

Truly belonging to the realm of parapsychology, there is no rational explanation for Nostradamus's predictive abilities, and yet there is no fakery involved. The manuscripts are genuine and readily available to scholars. His first book of prophecies contained some 354 four-line verses expressing his predictions, and several volumes followed. Nostradamus died in 1566, by which time he was held in high repute, or, as Robb put it, "a prophet with honor in his own country."

The prophecies extend from the 16th century until the middle of the fourth millennium, and Robb's work painstakingly points out those that have already been realized. Among other things, Nostradamus surpassed the widely marveled-at Jules Verne, as he foretold the invention of the periscope, submarine, airplane, the Montgolfier balloon, atomic warfare, and the coming of many wars and events that have become part of history. It would take an entire volume to list them all. During World War II, for example, "An old man with the title of chief will arise, of doddering sense . . . the country divided, conceded to gendarmes." Marshal Petain, Chief of State, was an old man when the Nazis made him ruler of a portion of divided France— the portion to be ruled by Vichy gendarmes!

It is a scientific axiom that if a large portion of a statement is correct, all of it *may well be* correct. Every prophecy made by Nostradamus between 1555 and 1566 pertaining to the period between then and today has come true. Not only were his prophecies specific, they also used terminology completely unknown at the time he made them. Around the middle of the 16th century, he spoke of communism, of aerial bombardments, of atom bombs, of submarines, and other ideas that came into being centuries later. He gave the name and profession of the assassin of a French king, an event that transpired in the following century.

There are a total of 942 prophecies. Famed Nostradamus scholar Dr. Alexander Centgraf, a German, has reassembled the deliberately mixed-up chronology of Nostradamus's verses. In 1968, Dr. Centgraf published these verses in their correct sequence. In one of the verses Nostradamus referred to the year 1607, in which the priests would be threatening astronomers because of their discoveries. As a matter of fact, it was in 1607 when a Dutchman by the name of Lippershey invented one of the first telescopes. Shortly thereafter, Galileo Galilei used this new instrument to discover that the Earth circles the sun and not vice versa. When he proclaimed this exciting new discovery, he came into conflict with the Church and was eventually forced to recant, even though he knew in his heart it was the truth.

Almost 300 years before the planet Neptune was actually discovered, Nostradamus predicted it and referred to the unknown planet by its present name, Neptune.

I am indebted to John Hogue, today's greatest Nostradamus scholar and author, for his help with a reference I consider of some importance in respect to recent world history; the terrible nuclear accident that occurred in the Ukraine at Chernobyl atomic energy plant in 1986 was one of the greatest disasters to befall Europe in decades. And even this, Nostradamus hinted at. In Nostradamus's epistle to King Henry II of France, there is reference to *fiel*, which means "bitter" in the French of Nostradamus's time. The line reading "le miel du fiel" likewise could be translated as "the passion or suffering of the 'bitter,'" and there "bitter" could then be a mask hiding the words "amoise amere" or "bitter herb." "Bitter herb of Artemis" is the French term for what we call wormwood, or, by extension, absinthe. "Chernobyl" in Russian means "wormwood." Thus, the reference to a future "suffering by wormwood (Chernobyl)."

Even more ominous is the mention of wormwood in the Apocalypse, the prophecies of St. John. Here there is no code, no disguise, and the term is plain. It only made sense, however, after the Chernobyl catastrophe had taken place.

Those who wish to delve into the prophecies of the great Nostradamus themselves will find a number of books on this intriguing subject listed in the Further Reading section.

Stainte Odile

There never was an age in the development of mankind and history, when prophets did not speak. Today, they are free and safe to do so without fear of being accused of witchcraft, or being in league with the devil.

Not so long ago, that would not have been possible, and prophecy was allowed and accepted only so long as it worked within the framework of the current state religion, whether Judaism, Christianity, or any other mainstream faith. While this inevitably inhibited the prophets somewhat, they also found a way to tell the truth (as they saw it) in such a way as to not offend authorities, yet get the message across to the world.

Sainte Odile, patron saint of Alsace, born in 657 A.D., is considered the source of a prophecy relating to a "bellicose Germany" and a "conqueror starting from the banks of the Danube who will win victories on land, by sea, and even in the air." This prophecy goes on to describe World War II in all detail. Whether this prophecy really stems from the 7th-century saint or is a later medieval prophecy simply attributed to her, it is definitely of very ancient origin.

Mother Shipton

The English seer, Mother Shipton, who lived around 1488, liked to express her prophecies in rhyme and verse. While some of her prophecies are open to varied interpretations, some are quite clear:

> *"Carriages without horses shall go*
>
> *and accidents fill the world with woe.*
>
> *Around the Earth thoughts shall fly*
>
> *in the twinkling of an eye."*

Edgar Cayce

Born in Hopkinsville, Kentucky in 1877, Edgar Cayce, husband, father, photographer, and Sunday school teacher, would become one of the most prolific and accurate prophets of all time, giving readings on everything from personal matters to world events and from spiritual philosophy to practical matters of health and healing.

Cayce became familiarly known as "the sleeping prophet" because of his ability to self-induce a deep trance state by lying down on a couch, eyes closed, from which state he was able to answer questions—from the profound to the mundane—on subjects about which he had no conscious knowledge.

From a young age, Cayce had been able to see visions, including recently dead relatives, with whom he was able to converse, and he had another uncanny knack: He was able to learn, via osmosis, simply by resting his head upon a book he wished to study and taking a nap!

According to Cayce himself, the information he gave was obtained in two ways. First, he was able, to a degree, to reach into the unconscious mind of the questioner for whom he was giving a reading. Other information he attributed to the so-called "Akashic Records," (from the Sanskrit, *akasha*, meaning "ether" or "all-pervading space"). To those who believe in its existence, this is a sort of universal data base containing all there is to be known about every thing and every individual, past, present, and future. To my knowledge, there has never been proof offered for the existence of these Records by any of its many proponents. It is far more likely that, with his mind in a relaxed state, Cayce—a powerful psychic to be sure—was simply better able to access all the information available from natural sources. We use such a small portion of our brain, and it's attribute, the mind, and as Aldous Huxley observed in his book *The Doors of Perception*, rather than being an organ of information *gathering*, our brain actually operates as a mechanism of *filtering*—that is, *inhibiting*—information that it discerns, according to its own criteria, is of no use to it. In all likelihood, Cayce was simply able to disengage the filtering aspect of his mind when in his "sleeping" or trance state.

Although he is most noted for his readings on the health ailments of those who sought his help (many of his suggested cures flew in the face of accepted medical science, yet proved effective and were subsequently studied, and many now are becoming mainstream), Cayce also spoke in trance about world affairs. The end of Communism and the United States and Russia becoming allies and friends was an unlikely situation when Cayce stated it, but of course it did occur. Christianization and democratization of Red China, also foreseen by Cayce, is yet to come, but the rising of Atlantis, the lost continent, while a reality to many of us, has not yet shown any sign of happening, especially by the date set by Cayce. There are, however, partial areas of it near the Florida coast waiting to be further explored.

Over his lifetime, Cayce gave more than 14,000 readings; these are archived in Virginia Beach, Virginia, at the Association for Research and Enlightenment, and have been studied by scholars and scientists in a variety of fields since the turn of the last century.

Just as with Nostradamus, whose prophecies I take very seriously, I regard Cayce's with utmost respect.

Malachy, van der Heide, and Other
Predictions of the Fates of the Popes

The power of the popes has always been shrouded in a kind of mystery, just as the "divine right of kings" has for many centuries kept rulers of sometimes-doubtful qualifications in power.

On a realistic level, the pope is nothing more than the Bishop of Rome and the head of the Roman Catholic Church, a man, inspired perhaps, but not a miracle worker. And yet, the enormous energies stemming from the religious faith of millions of people have endowed the papacy with almost supernatural status. No other head of a religious community shares that unique reputation, except perhaps the chief rabbi of some Hassidic sects believed by his followers to be the real Messiah.

Thus it is not surprising that prophets have commented upon the fate of the papacy for centuries. In the Middle Ages the popes were also temporal rulers—contrary to Jesus' kind of Christianity—and only in modern times have the popes of Rome retreated to their spiritual sanctuaries, where their position is unchallenged.

The fate of the papacy is of lesser impact now than it might have been 500 years ago, but its destiny, while no longer of geopolitical importance, has tremendous spiritual and moral implications for millions of people.

In the following pages, I am presenting precise prophecies regarding the Vatican and certain popes. There are amazing similarities between them, suggesting at the very least a common "source."

St. Malachy was a medieval abbot whose prophecies of doom foretold the end of the Vatican some 800 years ago—giving a description of every pope elected since that time. The reign of John Paul I was characterized as "of the waxing moon" and indeed his reign lasted just about one lunar cycle— only 34 days. John Paul II is referred to in the Malachy prophecies as "of the eclipse of the sun," and a more dramatic description of the Communist world can hardly be given from the Church's point of view.

According to Malachy's warnings, only three more popes remain before the Holy City vanishes at the death of Peter II, and Michael Nostradamus himself predicted the end of the Vatican in our time.

Jan Cornelis van der Heide lives in a small town in the Netherlands, and makes his living as an artist and sometime poet. From time to time, van der Heide has had visions about future events, many of which have already come true. Like the time he woke up and "saw my father with hands and face covered with blood, his head had gone through a pane of glass . . . his car totally wrecked." Two months later the accident occurred, but being forewarned, van der Heide somehow survived. The Dutchman claims that a long-dead monk inspires his many religious paintings, which have a strange, etheric quality to them. Perhaps because of his religious orientation, van der Heide was chosen to warn the world on September 13, 1978, that the newly elected Pope John Paul I "would not live long, but would die within four months."

In addition to this entry in his diary, van der Heide told a number of witnesses of the impending death of the newly elected Pope. All have signed affidavits to that effect. Stated R. la Grouw, of Joordwijk, Netherlands, a friend: "On Saturday September 16, 1978, I visited van der Heide's family. That evening, after Jan had read to us one of his poems about religion, he suddenly said, 'Pope John Paul will die suddenly within four months.'"

As the weeks passed, van der Heide felt more and more that the tragic event was not far off. On September 28, he decided to write to me, to reiterate his concern about John Paul I. That letter, sent off the following day, reached me several days later. But on the same afternoon, September 29, Pope John Paul I suddenly passed away. No sooner had a new pope been elected that Jan van der Heide's second sight tuned in on him.

"John Paul II will be involved in an airplane accident in a southern country, perhaps South America. It will be near dry, arid land with rocky soil and coast . . . the figures 1 and 8 suggest the year 1981." According to the Dutch seer, the new pope would show himself very orthodox and unyielding in matters of doctrine. Van der Heide wrote of all this on October 19, 1978. By now it is clear that he was right; the new Pope's unyielding stand on celibacy is well known. Van der Heide predicted that because of John Paul II's stand, more splinters will occur in the Church. Polarization will become more pronounced.

According to the Malachy prophecy, the Pope following John Paul I would come "from the eclipse of the sun"—an apt description of the Iron Curtain country of Poland. Apparently, the impact of what may well have been a fated event was so strong it penetrated the unconscious, psychic level of several other people. Bohdan Zacharko is a tool and die maker of Ukrainian descent, now living in Connecticut. On August 27, 1978, during mass, he suddenly had a vision. "I saw two coffins," he explained to me, "one opened and the other closed. . . . I seemed to be standing in front of the Vatican. I knew that the open coffin held John Paul I, but I could not see anything further of the closed coffin, except to the right I saw the towers of Moscow. From this I received the feeling that John Paul I would live only for a short while, and that his successor would not be Italian but Polish. I shared my vision with my coworkers and my family, but everyone laughed at me."

Edith Filliette has had ESP experiences all her life but never thought too much of them. Two years ago, however, she began to write them down as they occurred.

Educated in Europe and Canada, Miss Filliette worked as a writer for the *Readers Digest* and is now the direct mail promotion consultant, making her home in Massachusetts. In late July or early August, she had a "vivid dream" that left her very puzzled at the time.

> *"I was walking down a busy street somewhere in Europe, looking for transportation to the other side of town. I asked a woman passerby for directions. 'I know of a shortcut, but you must pass through the Polish embassy,' she*

replied. At the Polish Embassy I noticed a grand marble stairway winding up to another floor. I glanced upwards and saw three Catholic cardinals in full regalia coming down the stairway. I thought it was strange and at the same time I felt they were Cardinals from Poland and had come to the Embassy for some official papers. Two of the cardinals passed me without a look in my direction. But the third one stopped, looked straight at me as if he were trying to convey a message. He was very close, and I could see his face very distinctly.

"He was an attractive man of between 50 and 60, clean-shaven, with light or gray hair slightly protruding beneath the biretta, and a dignified and strong appearance. After some seconds of staring at me, he turned away and continued his walk downstairs, and I continued through the Polish Embassy, walking up the marble stairs, then through a long corridor, until I reached the 'other side of town.'

"There the dream ended."

As soon as news of the death of Pope Paul VI reached the world, Miss Filliette told two friends that the next pope might be Polish, and she described him. However, when John Paul I, an Italian, was chosen, she had the unmistakable feeling that a "mistake" had been made. Soon she was to learn how right she had been.

"The day John Paul I died," she explained, "I was hospitalized at the Massachusetts General Hospital in Boston. I did not know the pope had died during the night, and I was sitting up that particular morning around 6:45 a.m. Suddenly I heard an inner voice urging me: 'Turn on your TV . . . something important has happened.' I rejected the idea as I have an aversion to watching TV. But the voice returned more insistent 'Turn to number 5 and see what happened. . . .'

"I finally did, and there on the screen was Pope John Paul I and the announcement of his sudden death. At that moment I felt my dream had taken on meaning and that the next pope would indeed be Polish. I said so to a friend, and that he would be elected on October 16th."

Ms. Filliette's strange encounter with the unknown was not over by any means. Because she has no interest in Poland, nor any Polish relatives she knew nothing of any Polish cardinals as seen in her dreams. When the new pope was elected on October 16, as she had predicted, she was shocked to recognize his face: It was indeed the face she had seen!

Prophecies of World Events

Jan van der Heide has registered prophecies with me from time to time with the postmark guaranteeing the proper time reference. A great deal of this material refers mainly to Holland and people and situations of little impact for the world at large. But much of it is also relative to international conditions (some of these were also broadcast by Radio Veronica in the Netherlands), though a number have not come to pass:

> **November 23, 1980**: "Someone will shoot at President Reagan."
>
> **September 2, 1989**: "The Berlin Wall will come down." (This prediction was witnessed by radio journalist Marion Dietrich, originally from East Germany.)
>
> **November 18, 1989**: "People will try to kill President Gorbachev."
>
> **November 18, 1990**: "There will be a short and heavy war in the Middle East. I see American bombers above Baghdad."
>
> **November 18, 1990**: "Limited use of nerve gas by Iraq."
>
> **November 18, 1990**: "Gorbachev will disappear from the scene, in 1991. We will soon be able to read his memoirs."
>
> **January 18, 1991**: "Arafat will speak about peace with Israel in a short time."

All of these predictions came true in our time.

―•―〓◊〓―•―

Rosanna Rogers, of Cleveland and New York City, is a remarkably gifted professional psychic reader, whose knowledge of the tarot cards far exceeds that of any other tarot specialist, living or dead. Then, too, Rosanna uses some 220 cards of her own original design, whereas most everybody else uses the traditional 78 cards, although the deck's format and illustrations may vary. Now and again, Rosanna has a flash of prophecy, which she communicates to me, as well as other witnesses, and when the event predicted occurs, she reminds one and all of her prophetic statements.

Rosanna (Rogers by marriage) was born in Austria and brought up in Germany, where she attended high school at the Convent of the Sisters of St. Francis in Pirmasens, and College at the Covent of San Lioba, in Freiburg. She now lives in a colorful house in one of Cleveland's quiet districts on Svec Avenue, and has her own local cable television program. But people from many parts of the world keep reaching out to her for predictions. Over the years, Rosanna has sent me predictions or made them in my presence, or sometimes she has made them to reputable witnesses who have testified accordingly.

Some of the more outstanding ones:

January 10, 1990: "I see a 707 airplane, approaching the Atlantic coast, crashing. I perceive digits . . . 5?" (On January 26th, 1990, Columbian airliner, Flight 52, a 707, crashed near New York City.)

September 23, 1983: "The United States and the Soviet Union will recognize the need to work together in unison as the danger comes from nations with nothing to lose, such as Iran, Iraq, and Libya." (June–July.1990: The United States and Russia are chummy as never before, and their shared worries about Iraq and Iran are greater than ever.) How true the dangers in Iraq, as I write these lines in 2003!

July 19, 1973: "Nixon may get out of the Watergate Affair elegantly by resigning." (August 7, 1973: Nixon resigned.)

During the summer of 1989, Rosanna, whose accuracy I had been monitoring carefully for 13 years, insisted that all was not well with the president and his family. She insisted there were health problems and we would hear about them soon, and other problems even more worrisome, concerning his immediate family. Finally on January 10, 1990, she put her concerns in writing to me. How accurate was all this?

On February 15, 1990, Barbara Bush went through surgery on her lip and dealt with an eye problem; on January 29, Neil Bush, the president's son, started having serious business problems, sill mounting to ominous proportions; and on April 12, 1990, the president himself discovered signs of a serious disease.

Yolana Lassaw, usually only called by her first name (her mother's, actually, which she adopted for good luck years ago), is today the leading deep trance medium in America. In the tradition of Eileen Garrett, Ethel Johnson Meyers, and Trixie Allingham, to name but a few of those with whom I have worked with over the years, Yolana makes her living as a psychic reader available to clients for consultations about their private lives and future.

She has also become a busy adjunct to the police, giving freely of her time in the investigations of murder cases and missing persons in particular. I have taken part in some of these journeys, and she is truly on target.

Now and again she has prophetic visions and communicates them to me, as we are close friends, and close associates in this work for many years. Here are some of the precise prophecies by Yolana and their outcome:

> **November 12, 1978**: Yolana tells me of an impending railroad catastrophe, of a silver and blue train that would derail, with lots of injuries as a result. She saw this for late November or early December of that year. On December 3, the track Southern Crescent, en route to Washington from the South, derailed on a curve near Charlottesville, Virginia, killing six people and injuring 40.
>
> **December 17, 1978**: Yolana told me she foresaw a bombing at a busy New York terminal right after the New Year and that people would be hurt. She was convinced that it would be the work of a crazy person, not political. On, February 19, 1979, three teenagers set fire to a subway token booth, as a result of which three people died. The motive was personal revenge.
>
> **December 19, 1978**: Yolana spoke to me of an airplane crash "over hills or mountains in a suburban area," that there would be trouble with the left wing, and

there would be casualties. The figure 7 was also part of her vision. The following day a light plane crashed in a suburban area on the West Coast, the left wing hit a tree, and of the seven people involved, only one survived.

January 11, 1979: Yolana stated that "one oriental country would invade another very shortly." It so happened that on February 17, China surprised the world by invading Vietnam.

January 16, 1979: Yolana spoke of a "terror ride" on a train going to Coney Island. On February 26, a holdup man terrorized and victimized people on just such a train.

November 15, 1980: Yolana confided to her secretary, Rose Pannini, the gist of a vision, in which she saw someone in terrible danger near black gates: "A man gets out of a car, someone is going to be killed, it is very big—I hear many shots." She thought someone named David was involved. Three days before John Lennon was shot in front of the black gates of the Dakota Apartments in New York, by a man named Mark David Chapman, Yolana reported further on this vision that a name like "Lemon" kept running through her mind.

━━◆━━

While not exactly in the same league with Yolana and Rosanna Rogers, a pleasant lady from Brooklyn named Lucy Rivera has over the years proven to me her remarkable gift as a psychic. Primarily doing private readings that concerned the usual health, wealth, and love lives of individuals, it was startling to me that she unexpectedly did come up with spontaneous prophecies.

Lucy visited me on December 27, 1990, very concerned about a vision she had first had the previous year, in 1989. In the vision, she saw four airplanes over Manhattan, which she felt were threatening, and she connected this to the then ongoing struggle with Saddam Hussein of Iraq. But she also saw a bomb going off in the Wall Street area of Manhattan and smoke rising. The people involved she described as dark skinned people and wearing a kind of blue uniform like overalls, and she saw people running all over and great turmoil. She felt that the people who had caused this came from the Newark, New Jersey, area. The same basic vision reoccurred to her on January 15, 1991, and then she decided to see me about it so I could warn the authorities, which I did.

When the events failed to materialize during the Persian Gulf crisis, I thought no more about it, until the terrible World Trade Center bombing took place two years later. The perpetrators, now jailed for life, did indeed include some that came from New Jersey, and the overalls were work clothes worn by them as they were posing as a kind of repair crew when entering the building; they were dark skinned people.

Furthermore, in the prophetic mind of the psychic person, where time, as we know it, does not exist, two events became one. In addition to the bombing, Rosanna also saw the airplanes. Even though the four planes in her vision appeared in the same location, when the second event occurred on September 11, 2001, there were, in fact, four planes involved on the day of the World Trade Center tragedy (although one targeted the Pentagon, and one crashed in Pennsylvania, due to intervention by passengers and crew).

◆—◆ ≍ ◈ ≍ ◆—◆

Prophecy, then, is neither to be ignored, nor feared. As prophets are humans, subject to failure in even the very best of cases, one should consider prophecies as possibilities rather than an inevitable, accomplished fact in our future. The higher level of destiny places any one of use at a place and in a time where that person is meant to be. Time, as we know it, is only a convenience and not an absolute, certainly nonexistent in a timeless dimension beyond this one.

Only by acknowledging a higher order governing our destinies can we come to terms with prophecy. But it would be prudent to base our actions on an assumption that a dire prophecy may well take place as predicted—in the sense that we can and must abort them by sheer willpower, by spiritual/moral renewal of our lives, and by the actions we take in this, our mundane world. Catastrophes involving human beings are the result not only of divine will (to test us, perhaps) but very much of human action—for, or against, as the case may be. Each prophecy must be dealt with individually, and on its own merits, ultimately not because other prophecies by the same prophet have already been fulfilled.

Ours is a less than perfect world, and evil is rampant, evil expressed by us, the humans. The power of prayer and spiritual renewal can and will influence the outcome of events, and we cannot really know which prophecy will be fulfilled as made, and which may yet be averted. That, too, is part of the karmic system, to encourage our efforts to alter outcomes in efforts toward preventing evil and destruction in our world.

CHAPTER 4

DREAMS AND THE PSYCHIC

Because the conscious mind is inactive when we sleep, much psychic material, or information, if you will, works its way into our awareness through our dreams. But there are dreams and *dreams*: Some are merely expressions of unfulfilled desires, anxieties, or simply the result of too much indulgence at dinner. Shakespeare refers to "the stuff that dreams are made of," but never comes to grips with the nature of the dream itself.

Eastern mystics are sure that all dreams are prophetic and must be interpreted symbolically, and ever since the arrival of psychoanalysis in the early part of the last century, dream material has been co-opted by the medical fraternity, pored over for clues to both physical ailments and mental disturbances.

As with all beliefs, there is some truth in dream theories, but not all the truth. The difficulty of explaining the nature of dreams satisfactorily in terms of modern scientific thought lies in the fact that a dream is not an experience in itself; a dream is a condition in which several types of experiences may occur. In other words, just as walking depends for its significance largely on who walks, where he walks, or how he walks, so dreaming is not by itself an absolute condition. It's important that we not slip into the superstitious mode of ancient times, when each and every dream was considered to hold prophetic meaning, but to strike a balance in our observation of dreams for the various types of information they may hold.

The kinds of dreams that seem to foretell the future, prophetic dreams, are of a particular kind. Prophetic dreams, to begin with, often seem to be far clearer than ordinary dreams, which come to us often in confused symbols, or scenes that seem to make no sense at all. Also, while ordinary dreams are quickly forgotten on awakening, the true psychic dream tends to impress us and stay with us for hours if not days. It may be a message about the future, or a present problem, or a warning, but it is usually very clear and concise.

Joe dreamt that his brother Carl, whom he had not seen in more than 12 years, would suddenly pop up again, even though he had no idea where Carl lived, having lost contact with his elder brother several years before. Sure enough, two weeks after the dream, there was Carl, big as life, wanting Joe to know he had remarried and to meet his new wife, after their long estrangement.

Dotty K. dreamt that her brand new car had been stolen, and she even saw the street corner where it all happened. But she thought it was just her worries about the car, which had cost her a lot more money than she could afford. The next morning as she drove to work, she needed to accomplish an errand that would involve her parking her car on the street for a short time. Suddenly, she recognized the spot—the very corner she had seen in her dream the night before! She did not ignore the matter, but moved her car to a nearby garage. Would the car have been stolen? Dotty did not want to find out!

Dreams, "the gateway to the unconscious," are very subjective and personal. But because dreams are so universally considered to be, at times, portents of things to come, it is important to understand exactly what dreaming is all about.

We all dream—every night—even though sometimes we do not remember our dreams.

Four Types of Dreams

Assuming that the dream covers a multitude of situations, it appears that there are four main classifications, which I will go on to detail. Examining these categories, it will become clear that the dream state is simply a more convenient and flexible form of awareness than is the waking state. The limitations imposed by the time-space continuum of the waking state have no meaning during the dream state, in which the physical body is temporarily excluded from participation in the experience.

Since the *etheric* body experiences on the thought plane, in which physical and time barriers are removed, the experience is the more immediate and stronger.

1. Dreams Caused by Physical Conditions

These dreams include nightmares and anxiety dreams, to name a couple. A typical example is the man who overeats and then has illogical nightmares. The anxiety states are induced by malfunction of the biochemical system of the body, with pressures creating the false dream image. Illness and high fever can induce similar effects.

In such dreams we find ourselves in a state of fear or upset. Something we have not resolved during our waking hours continues to bother us during our sleep when the conscious mind is not operating and the unconscious mind, the free and sometimes unrestrained part of our personality, has the power to impress us. Anxiety dreams are natural and normal parts of our daily lives and not necessarily an indication of illness or the need to spend long hours and much money with psychoanalysis (which, more often than not, does not really help resolve the underlying problem).

A typical anxiety dream might be that you are on a train, bus, or airplane, or tying to catch one and being very worried about missing it. Or you are already on board but your luggage is not, or the luggage is and you are still outside worried about losing it. Such dreams occur to many people from time to time and do not mean you are about to travel somewhere. Instead, the train (or bus or plane) represents your ongoing life, your progress into the future, and the dream is giving voice to a fear of not getting on or losing future security—whether work-related or personal security. It is a very common dream.

Another dream often reported to me involves finding yourself back in school or in your youth, at a time when you did not yet have full responsibility for yourself. On the one hand, fear of not doing well in school would indicate basic insecurity with your work performance today. On the other hand, dreaming of a time when all was serene in your life, and your parents took care of your needs, might reflect a deep desire not to face up to present-day difficulties in your life—sort of a dream escape into a simpler yesterday.

A dream in which the boss visits your house unexpectedly, finding you thrilled by the visit, yet also embarrassed because you are unprepared, might be interpreted as a desire to advance at your job, a desire for a raise perhaps, but an uncertainty as to whether you deserve it or if you should ask.

There is a kind of dream, better perhaps called a *nightmare*, which is caused by physical discomfort or illness of the body. The nightmare dream can be triggered by anything from a cold and fever, to indigestion, to being too hot or too cold in bed. Or it can be caused by having earlier witnessed something traumatic, for instance, a horror movie or a real accident—anything that would have been frightening in real life and usually not long before the nightmare comes on. Obviously, if you dream of monsters devouring you, or of experiencing some kind of violence, such as being in a shipwreck, drowning in the ocean, or being pursued by anything ranging from murderous people to demons and devils with horns, you are having a classical nightmare. Frequently it also involves a kind of pressure on your chest, and the very name *nightmare* derives from the old superstitious belief that such dreams were caused by an invisible horse sitting your chest!

Truly bizarre dreams of this kind should not be taken seriously as anything other than what they are. If you search your memory as to what you experienced the day before, you will find the explanation for what has caused your unconscious mind—which is pure emotions and cannot reason things out—to react so violently. Eating heavily within two hours before bedtime can easily cause such dreams, as can a variety of fever-inducing illnesses. There are also some medically prescribed drugs, from stimulants to painkillers to tranquilizers that can cause such wild, irrational dreams images.

2. Dreams of a Prophetic Nature

Dreams of this nature may include clairvoyant and warning dreams, prophecies, and other psychic experiences. In the case of psychic dreams, details are always remembered after awakening and generally retained for long periods (contrary to other kinds of dreams). These can be of two types: a warning in the form of premonition or projection of danger ahead, or it can be simply a prophetic dream in which you clearly foresee future events, which may be of quite a mundane nature. When you experience a psychic dream, be sure to notice whether you are the outside observer of events or actually in the picture. If you are outside, chances are it is a warning and not final, but if you are "in the movie" better take heed and be careful.

There is also a relatively rare experience of dreaming of a past life. If a dream is truly one of a past life, it will be very specific in details of place, time, and names, and quite possibly will become a *recurrent dream* with little change in the scenario. Such experiences can be followed up through hypnotic regression, which I have done in valid cases with frequent success, expanding upon the information to where it can actually be verified from research sources.

Dr. Hornell Hart of Duke University has done a great deal of laboratory work analyzing the incidence of precognitive dreams among average people. It has been found statistically true that almost everybody dreams, but that most people do not remember their dreams. It also has been found that precognition is a fairly common occurrence. Tested and confirmed examples of clairvoyant dreams exist by the thousands in the files of universities and psychical research societies. That a person may experience a future event long before it actually occurs is not a matter for speculation. It is a proven fact. It is also a most challenging fact, for what are we to make of our free will if the future already exists somewhere along time?

3. Dreams in Which the Dreamer Travels

In these generally vivid dreams, the dreamer seems to be in a strange place, perhaps among people he or she does not know (or, possibly, among familiar folks), at a physical distance from where his or her body lies sleeping. This phenomenon is commonly known as *astral projection* or out-of-body experiences (OOBEs).

These dreams are often remembered rather clearly, and the experiences lack the confusion and illogical associations so common to the first category. In fact, in this type of dream, the dreamer often thinks he or she isn't dreaming at all, but is really there. In these dreams, people find themselves in distant places, see, and even talk to strange people or good friends. In many cases of this type, the individuals who were visited in the dreamer's dream state have verified that they had been visited! To them, commonly, the visitor (the dreamer) seemed their usual self, only to disappear into thin air when challenged or spoken to.

I recently met a man who dreamed he was in a Turkish bath, where the attendant asked him for his papers. Replying that he had no papers, the man desired to leave the unpleasant situation at once. Immediately he found himself back in his own bed. The following day, chance had it that a friend of his took him to the same Turkish bath. There stood the attendant our dreamer had argued with in his dream state. When the attendant saw the man, he angrily pounced on him and again demanded his papers. Also, he wanted to know how he had so suddenly disappeared from under his very nose!

What actually happens in *these* dream states—called astral projection or astral travel—(usually involuntary, but occasionally produced at will), will be more fully discussed in the next chapter.

4. Psychoanalytical Dreams

To the psychoanalyst, all dreams have symbolic and analytical meanings. I am convinced that many dreams have these types of meanings, but not all of them. Freud thought that all dream images were sexually motivated. Jung and his disciples came to think differently. The sign of the true analytical dream is that the dreamer does things he cannot do in real life, solves problems he cannot solve when awake, or experiences conditions and situations he secretly desires but has been unable to experience, whether because of worldly restrictions or because of mental and/or emotional blocks. In this type of dream, the dreamer is the main character, and everything else revolves around him. In the other dream categories, he is more of an observer or visitor.

From time immemorial, dreams were thought by most religions to be a state in which God could manifest directly to the sleeper and bring him messages or orders that would not reach him during the more prosaic daylight hours. The Bible is full of these incidents, from Moses and the prophets of old to the New Testament.

Clearly, then, two out of four categories of dreams are not properly a subject for the psychiatrist, or psychoanalyst, but belong in the realm of parapsychology. Precognition is the explanation for one group, and out-of-body experiences for the other. But even the psychic dream group may contain both precognitive information and material suggestive of reincarnation memories.

What these two groups do not present is any connection with conventional dream material suggestive of symbolism, suppressed feelings, or unresolved trauma.

—•—————•—

We have come a long way from simplistic dream interpretation, whether Dr. Sigmund Freud's sexually tinged way of explaining all dreams, or, on the other extreme, Gypsy fortune-tellers' ridiculous, often frightening, and largely invalid interpretations of their meanings. Dreams can be an important entry to our own psychic potentials. By learning to distinguish between the various types of dreams, one can not only understand one's self better, but also profit from possible warnings or glimpses into the future.

A woman in Virginia reported a dream, or rather a sequence of dreams, which seem to defy the ordinary laws of time and space. Not that this is an isolated instance for her by any means; dreaming *true* is part and parcel of her daily life. She has taken her special gift in stride, however.

At the time when John F. Kennedy, still a senator, was running for election as president, the lady was an active campaign worker, the only time in her life she had ever become involved in political work. She had never met the candidate, but felt his goals sufficiently worthwhile to help with the campaign on a local level.

About that time she had a series of extraordinary dreams, all the same night. In the first dream, she saw herself enter a large room through an open door, with the feeling she had been chosen for a particular task. There was a desk, with an empty chair in front of it. But a man was seated on the corner of the desk; he seemed very relaxed and smiled at her. He was dressed in a black suit and white shirt; his tie was black and white. His shoes were black. As his legs were crossed, she noticed that he also wore white socks. In short, he was Kennedy. As she observed, Kennedy turned his head and looked toward the other side of the room. There was a woman there, Mrs. Kennedy, seemingly suspended in midair, and dressed in sheer black fabric, which was billowing and blowing around her like clouds. She looked at Kennedy, both smiled and nodded their heads as if in secret agreement, then both looked at the dreamer. At that point, the lady from Virginia awoke.

Returning to sleep, she found herself back in the same room, which now was dark though it had been sunlit before. Waking up again, the dreamer went back to sleep a third time. Again, she found herself in a room, but a different one this time. A well-dressed man in his 30s was guiding her around the large room, and, to her surprise, she noticed the president's mother seated at a desk. She was then led to another desk and made to understand that it was for her, the dreamer. At that point, the dream ended.

Several years later, the lady saw Kennedy when he stopped in her town while campaigning. As she stood close to his plane, Kennedy smiled at her, and came toward her with outstretched hand. But something made her run away from the handshake, and as she looked back toward the president she saw once again the billowing black she had seen in her dream!

What is extraordinary is the fact she had what we call a recurrent dream, but all in the same night. The purpose of this "message" was to impress her with the importance of the dream message. But the black clothes of Mrs. Kennedy and of his mother make it clear that this was a prediction regarding Kennedy's death.

Normally, dreams that are true precognitive dreams (and clearly remembered the next day) contain important facts and in this case, the dreamer could have sent off a warning to the president. But realizing her marginal relationship to him, she did not. "Recurrent" dreams should never be ignored and the message in them should be made known to the principal figure in the dreams.

Out-of-Body Experiences

An out-of-body experience (OOBE), also called *astral projection*, is the result when the bond between the physical body and the astral, or etheric body, which is the seat of the personality, is weakened. The personality then wanders off, finds himself drawn to various places and people, and, being fully conscious except for the absence of a physical body, acts and reacts as if nothing were unusual about his appearance. In this state, distance, as we know it, is of no consequence, and it takes only a fraction of a second to cover thousands of miles. A similar condition exists when the same bonds are permanently cut at the moment of death, and apparitions of the deceased are seen by distraught relatives at some distance. An experimental form of this separation of physical (outer) and etheric (inner) body is called *distant viewing*, but in essence, all these terms mean the same thing. Thousands of such cases are on record and are fully documented.

OOBEs most frequently happen during sleep, during dream states. However, unlike many types of dreams, during the OOBE, the dreamer has almost total control over his movements, because his logical mind is functioning properly during the projection. I say *almost*, because it takes great discipline to control the thoughts that can propel the personality all over the globe at the very moment of desire. When the dreamer wishes to return to his bed, he so *thinks,* and instantly finds himself back home.

Many people have reported a strong sensation of falling from great heights and/or a sense of dizziness just before awakening. This is due to the sudden and rather sharp stepping down, or slowing down, of one's bodily vibrations from the thinner and much faster etheric plane to the denser, and therefore slower, physical one. The sensation of slowing down is commonly expressed in a "falling" dream. Astral projections are common and not in the least harmful other than a little tiredness after awakening. But then, all travel is tiring, after all.

Once we realize and accept as fact the duality of our body (and the trinity of our personality), all of these phenomena become easy to understand. Our physical body covers a lighter, inner duplicate body, and when the outer, heavier, physical "shell" is dissolved at death you simply inhabit the inner duplicate body without so much as a hitch (unless there are emotional factors preventing it). The only noticeable difference between being "alive" and being now "dead" is the absence of the notion and feeling of time, the absence of pain and illness. Now you are in a world that looks very much like the one you just left, and you will find some relatives or friends who have gone on before you and are now there to welcome you into this new environment.

But you can also temporarily leave your physical shell behind though you remain connected to it by a cord (the so-called "silver cord"). Otherwise you will indeed have "passed over."

This temporary separation of the two bodies you inhabit, one way or the other, can be caused by a number of circumstances. It may occur during surgery, when you have been given a chemical to put you to sleep to prevent your feeling pain; a number of people under anesthesia have, as a result, also had near-death experiences (more about these in Chapter 8), or found themselves able to observe every detail of the operation being performed on their physical, outer body, and have been able to report these details accurately after waking. Such is the case of Mrs. Elaine L., of Washington state, who reported to me an experience she had at the dentist's office at the age of 16:

> *"I had suffered several days from an infected back tooth and because my face was badly swollen, our dentist refused to remove the tooth until the swelling subsided.*

Shortly after the Novocaine was administered, I found myself floating close to an open window. I saw my body in the dental chair and the dentist working feverishly. Our landlady, Mrs. E., who had brought me to the dentist, stood close by, shaking me and looking quite flabbergasted and unbelieving. My feeling at the time was of complete peace and freedom. There was no pain, no anxiety, not even an interest in what was happening close to that chair. Soon I was back to the pain and remember, as I left the office, that I felt a little resentful. The dentist phoned frequently during the next few days for assurance that I was all right."

But some people can have such out-of-body experiences (or astral projections) during sleep and may mistake for a dream what is, in fact, a journey out of the body during which they observe objective reality and will recall it on awakening. There is nothing unusual or dangerous about this.

Traveling clairvoyance or distant viewing simply directs one's inner body in definite direction and is most likely to occur during planned experiments.

Skilled deep trance mediums are capable of "bringing through" a discarnate person by letting that person use their physical bodies and speech mechanism to converse with a client in this way. Normally the deep trance medium will have a guide to control everything, including the duration of this "visit." Under no circumstances must the client, or sitter, touch the body of the entranced medium or take any kind of physical action interfering with this process.

It is regrettable that so much misinformation about trance and mediumship is still about, due to some extent to the emphasis put on ESP as the sole source of a psychic's ability to predict the future or perform in any way involving paranormal abilities. This is also the result of the uneasy feelings most researchers in parapsychology have had for many years toward anything hinting at the existence of a very real Other Side of Life that they felt had religious connotations, but in fact it does not. Happily, today's parapsychologists are more and more coming around to the realization that we do have two complete sides to our lives, both tangible, but of differing density.

Psychic Healing

Psychic ability can take many forms, and one of the most valuable is the gift of energy healing, which can occur in anyone, either as a single aspect of an array of developed psychic skills belonging to that individual, or alone.

The phenomenon of psychic energy healing is as old as mankind itself. It may be defined as the identification of and the treatment of ailments, both physical and mental, by the powers of the spirit, or, at any rate, by forces that man has not yet recognized as being physical in the ordinary sense.

Early psychic healing was done mainly by shamans, priests or lay priests, and it was thought necessary to surround the application of such healing with a certain mystery in order to strengthen the patient's belief in it, and thus strengthen his will to get well. To this very day, it makes a great deal of difference whether a sick person trusts his doctor or not. Perhaps faith cannot move mountains, but it can surely rally the body's own defense mechanisms.

In psychic healing, no medicines of any kind are used, and it is not necessary that the patient be a believer for the cure to work. Certainly faith helps—and also strengthens the resistance to disease—but true psychic healing, which is often instantaneous or very nearly so, does not require such state of mind on the part of the subject. There are several kinds of what is often referred to as "unorthodox healing" in England—as if there were such a thing as orthodox pathology and unorthodox—depending on the method used.

The basic difference between conventional medicine and the various forms of psychic healing has been summed up recently by Dr. William McGarey, a medical doctor who heads the Edgar Cayce Clinic in Phoenix, Arizona, where treatments according to Cayce are available.

"The way Cayce looks at it," Dr. McGarey explained to me, "an individual is first of all a spiritual being and manifests, through mind, as a material being. The spirit creates, and the physical body is the result. But in medicine, we think of structure—a person has liver disease, or lung disease. The way Cayce sees illness is that one of the forces within the body has become unbalanced with the other forces."

What Exactly Is Psychic Healing?

A lot of confusion exists in the mind of the average person as to what psychic healing is and how it comes about . . . if it comes about. If one is to grasp the significance of these seemingly impossible cures, one has to accept the duality of man as the rational basis—a physical body on the outside, but a finer, inner, or etheric, body underneath, which is the seat of the real persona, the soul, if you wish. Psychic healing is always holistic. The entire person is healed, body and etheric body; one without the other cannot be treated.

There are a number of healing processes that differ from *currently* accepted medical practice. They are as old as man, and have existed in various forms and under various names since time immemorial. In ancient times, such healings were considered miraculous (or sometimes diabolic) and only in recent years has an orderly, reasonable scientific approach been possible. Today, more and more members of the medical profession are taking another look at these seemingly "impossible" cures, when a scant five or 10 years ago, the subject could not even be discussed with them.

First, there is psychic healing *proper*. Here the healer draws energy from his physical body, mainly from the two centers called solar plexus—one in back of the stomach, and one at the top of the head—where ganglia of nerves come together. This energy is then channeled through his or her hands and applied to the aura (the magnetic field extending somewhat beyond the physical body) of the patient, which is also the etheric or inner body. A discolored aura indicates illness, and a good healer will notice any areas of discoloration. As the healer places his or her energy into the troubled areas of the aura, diseased particles are displaced and a vacuum is momentarily created. Into this vacuum, healthy electrically charged particles push to fill the gap in the aura, and instant healing of the inner body is the result, since the integrity of the physical body is dependent upon and in conformity with its inner etheric counterpart.

This type of psychic healer—either a man or a woman, sometimes even a youngster, for the gift plays no favorites—rarely touches the patient's skin. The healing takes place at the periphery of the aura, where it is most sensitive. The healing may take place whether the patient believes in it or not. It is a purely mechanical process and its success depends on the healer's ability to draw enough of his life force into his hands to affect the patient's energetic component.

James Douglas DePass, of Atlanta, Georgia, an author and officer of the local chapter of the Theosophical Society, consulted Betty Dye, a psychic healer, in Atlanta. Mrs. Dye, a simple housewife who had the gift, wasn't told anything about the visitor's complaints. Immediately, she went into a state of trance, during which one of her so-called controls (guides), who had been a medical doctor while in the flesh, diagnosed Mr. DePass's ailment as stomach trouble. Speaking through the medium, but in a voice of his own, the doctor from Beyond then placed Mrs. Dye's hands on Mr. DePass's stomach. Although DePass had been in continual pain right up to his arrival (he suffered from unexplained stomach trouble and nausea) the pains left *immediately* after the treatment. He walked out, a well man, free from further pain in the days to come.

Mrs. Floyd Cummings went to Betty Dye in a state of abject fear: Her doctor had told her she had a growth in her throat and surgery was necessary. As Mrs. Cummings tells it, "The day before surgery I went to see Betty Dye, who gave me psychic healing. During the treatment I experienced a wonderful feeling of cleansing, and extreme heat coming from the hands of the medium while in trance. When I went to the doctor afterwards, the growth had completely disappeared and has not come back since."

Betty Dye is one of perhaps a dozen reputable psychic healers in this country who have been gaining a reputation of helping where conventional medicine can't. But it is the earmark of the reliable psychic healer that the patient feels the "heat" of the healer's energized hands.

———◆———

Dr. John Myers, a dentist from London, had, for years, tried to organize psychic healers into an association as he knew it in his native England, but he never succeeded. He was much more successful in healing, however. R. L. Parish, an American businessman who was suffering from a chronic sciatic condition as well as from near-blindness without hope of a cure, had been sent to Myers as a last resort. A few days after Myers treated him, Parish was totally without pain for the first time in years, and was able to discard his heavy eye glasses.

Interestingly, Myers was even able to heal himself, something few psychic healers can do. In 1957 he suffered a serious hemorrhage and was rushed to Medical Arts Hospital in New York in the middle of night. A panel of specialists agreed that Myers had a growth near the right kidney and an immediate operation was in order if Myers was to survive. But the psychic healer refused and informed his doctors he would do for himself what he had often done for others. He remained in the hospital for one week, concentrating on his own healing. By the end of that week, the growth had disappeared, and Myers went home. The following year, he came down with an acute inflammation of the appendix, a condition that can be fatal if not immediately attended to. Again, Myers refused an operation. Two hours later, all pain had ceased and an examination revealed that the inflammation had completely disappeared! Myers had his appendix to the end of his long life.

＊—+　二〇二　+—＊

But truly rivaling the healing results of the late Edgar Cayce, and far outshining any more recent paranormal healers is the Israeli healer Ze'ev Kolman. He has cured cancer and heart disease, permanently, and treated people with such serious illnesses as multiple sclerosis and even paralysis.

Kolman uses bioenergetic power, by passing his palms over the body of the patient. He has also been quite successful with absent healing via the telephone, in one case curing a woman in Japan with 10 long distance sessions. The sound of his voice relayed through the telephone was just as successful as if I had been coming from Kolman to a patient in his physical presence. The feats of Ze'ev Kolman, who lives in New York City, are well documented with medical reports and laboratory statements, backing up his cures.

Physical Healing

The second kind of unorthodox treatment works through actually touching of the body in the afflicted areas. This "laying on of hands" has been practiced by many religions, and even today it is at least symbolically part of church ritual. Although the prime force in this kind of treatment is still the psychic energy of the healer, a positive attitude toward it on the part of the patient is helpful, and when the healer is also a priest or minister, religious faith enters the process to some extent.

Dean Kraft, originally a musician from Brooklyn, works with medical doctors and often goes into hospitals to minister to patients (with their doctors' approval). Kraft discovered his supernormal abilities by accident, as it were, in November, 1972:

> He was driving home from work, when he heard a strange, clicking sound and found doors locked though he had not touched the buttons. He asked, more as a joke than seriously, if there were spirits present, and, to his amazement, received an answer in a sort of code of clicks. At the time, he was working in a music shop, and together with his boss, he perfected this code until he could actually communicate with them.
>
> One day, he heard the horrible sounds of an automobile crash outside the shop. He rushed to the street and found a woman on the pavement who had been badly hurt. Something told him to hold her in his hands until an ambulance came to take her to the hospital. Later, when he drove home, the unseen communicators told him, via the click code, "tonight your hands were used for healing."
>
> He did not understand the message, but when he checked on the woman's condition, the hospital told him she was on the critical list and would undergo surgery in the morning. Placing a telephone call the next day to find out how she was doing after the surgery, he was shocked to hear she had been discharged. Somehow her injuries had healed themselves during the early hours of the morning, he was told.

Hypnotherapy

In this form of psychic healing, hypnosis is induced in the patient so that he or she may effect self-healing in this state. The healer first explores any emotional conflicts within the patient, has the patient remove them (via suggestion), and replaces them with positive, helpful suggestions. By placing low-key commands into the unconscious mind of the patient, the hypnotic suggestions enable the patient to use his or her own psychic energies to overcome whatever ailment may be troubling them.

Faith Healing

Often confused in the public's mind with psychic healing, faith healing actually has little in common with this other method. In faith healing everything depends on three elements. First, the afflicted person must have a religious belief in the power of healing (and intercession of divine forces), the more fanatical, the better. Second, the patient must have unlimited confidence in the healer from whom he expects "the miracle," and third, a large audience (the larger the better) vastly improves the chances that the faith healing will succeed.

The works of the late Katherine Kuhlman are prime examples of faith healing. Kuhlman never took credit for the considerable number of cures taking place right in front of the crowd, but hinted at divine will working through her as the originator of the seeming miracle.

But successful faith healings are not necessarily the results of religious belief alone. In invoking spiritual guidance, the faith healer, first of all, unleashes within him- or herself energetic forces that are utilized to heal the sick; the expectant state in which the usually desperate patient finds himself, often to the point of hysteria, in turn spurs his own healing powers to higher performance, and so the result may be a spontaneous cure. The reservoir of human psychic energy represented by the large audience is also drawn upon to supply additional power for the process.

Occasionally, faith healing can also work *without* an audience.

Cecile Diamond, age 14, suffered from inflammation of the brain. Doctors gave her one chance in a hundred of survival. Rabbi Solomon Friedlander, a spiritual healer,

*placed an amulet in Cecile's hand and prayed. The next
day the girl felt better, and was able to leave the hospital soon after, completely cured. With her own desperate desire to be healed, as well as her confidence in her
religious beliefs, the rabbi accomplished the healing.*

It is important to know how healing works, and the various forms
it takes, because professional healers are by no means the only ones
who can help the sick. Many ordinary people who are psychic also
possess psychic healing powers and use them. This should be encouraged so long as there is a balance between conventional medical check-
ups and healing so that we may use the best of both worlds together.

Psychic healing is related to out-of-body experiences only in that
the healer must first heal the inner, etheric body before the outer,
physical duplicate will feel the effect.

Both in OOBEs and psychic healing, we do not deal in any way
with the physical, outer body, which is expected to fall in line with the
healing of the inner body once that is accomplished.

Orthodox medicine knows nothing of the inner body. It applies its
remedies, treatments, and potions strictly to the physical, outer body.
This is especially true when conventional medicine fails and psychic
healing works.

CHAPTER 6

CHANNELING AND PAST LIVES

Just as fashion plays a role in conventional medicine—sometimes a larger role than science—certain paranormal practices or beliefs also occur in cyclical trends. After World War I, the bereaved frequented spiritualist séances in droves, in the hope their loved ones would talk with them from the Great Beyond. And sometimes they did.

Fraud was easily detected if the alleged communicator could not be properly identified by the relative or friend at the séance. To this day, a certain amount of material coming through in spiritualist circles is valid. The proof lies always in the specific nature of the material or message, and if only generalities are obtained, buyer beware.

Channeling is the latest permutation of this fad, which arose during the 1970s and has had some staying power. In fact, it is still with us, even if some of the people purporting to practice it haven't the vaguest idea what it is.

Trance Mediumship

Ever since I worked in the field now called parapsychology, going back at least 30 years, I had been familiar with an ability of some psychics commonly called trance mediumship. Trance mediumship, in technical terms, involves the dissociation of the medium's (that is, the psychic's) personality from his or her body and the takeover of that now empty body (or *instrument*, as the medium's body is called) by an alleged exterior or foreign personality—generally one who has passed over—for the purpose of speaking with the living. Depending on exact and individual circumstances, such as background or education of the medium, test conditions, and supervision of the experiment, any messages or information conveyed in this way will be regarded as veridical or not. Among researchers, there are those who reject any notion of dead people speaking through the living, regardless of the evidence pointing in that direction. Other researchers, including myself, interpret the authenticity of such phenomena strictly on the basis of results: If the material obtained through a trance medium is accurate in terms of later verification, unknown or inaccessible to the medium at the time of the experiment, and sufficiently precise and detailed, any reasonable researcher will accept it as prima facie evidence in the absence of any strong evidence to the contrary.

Trance mediums are rare. Why this should be so, I don't know, except, perhaps, because the work does seem to be very strenuous in physical terms. Nobody who has worked for many years with physical mediums (which includes trance mediums as well as that even rarer phenomenon, ectoplasmic manifestations) will doubt that the medium undergoes extreme stress while working, and no actress can fake what transpires in front of the experienced researcher.

Ever since the 19th century when spiritualism was in its heyday, in place of what today is called parapsychology (which has a far more stringent sets of rules, to be sure), the communication with the dead through the instrument of the trance medium has been studied, recorded, and published. Mainly in England and later in Boston, and then in New York, the Societies for Psychical Research took these experiments very seriously and it is a pity so little of this kind of study is done today under conditions eliminating fraud and deception.

But as trance mediums tended to work more with private clients eager to hear from a loved one passed over, or with the police in providing valuable clues to murder cases—sometimes obtained, allegedly, from the victim directly (and sometimes with good results), most psychical researchers preferred the lab and the tedious testing of ESP, based on the postulated need of repeatability of the experiment before accepting the phenomena as genuine.

It has always been my contention that the lab and repeatability prove little if anything, whereas competent, repeated, and careful observation of actual, natural phenomena, if and when they occur in life, yields real clues and scientific data.

Messages From Masters

Then along came the channelers. On the surface, they looked and acted like trance mediums. They closed their eyes or rolled them dramatically, before going into their particular state. Shortly thereafter a voice pretending to be someone other than the channeler would speak to the audience or client. Now the difference between this process when a genuine trance medium does it and when a channeler does it, is of course not the outward show, but what comes out of the channeler's mouth.

Channeling has become not only big business, including more than in-person seminars where the faithful gather and, at a stiff price, are allowed to partake of the often questionable pearls of wisdom dropping from the lips of their channeler, but also audio tapes, magazines, follow-up books, more seminars, and question and answer sessions where people seek the counsel of the channeling entity in solving their personal problems.

Perhaps the kingpin of them all, in my opinion, is a crafty lady using the name of J. Z. Knight, and claiming to be the spokeswoman (channel) for one "Ramtha," whom she has characterized as a native of India who lived 35,000 years ago. Anyone familiar with Indo-Germanic language roots will know that the name Ramtha (really, Ramatha) could not have existed 35,000 years ago. The people whose language may have contained that term were still unborn in what, some 15,000 to 20,000 years later, became known as the Pamir plateau, north of India. Much of the style used by Mrs. Knight in her Ramtha personality reminds one of Edgar Cayce, the granddaddy of trance communication, whom dozens upon dozens of would-be mediums have claimed as their inspiration, if not actual communicator. And just as with the Cayce material, eager groups of followers gathered at all these readings, most prolifically produced during the 1980s, and tried to interpret them in such a way that they might present a new, world-shaking approach to life. It was a setup for disappointment. Any fairly intelligent person, with a smattering of psychology and religious orientation, could come up with similar advice. You don't have to be 35,000 years old to do it.

But let us assume for the moment that there really was an entity speaking through Mrs. Knight, a real person long deceased, as some of the so-called guides do, with many reputable trance mediums. Would it not be sensible to establish that we are hearing from an "enlightened one" (as Ramtha repeatedly called himself), who actually lived at one time or other in a place on this planet? Well, if we can't find his name listed in a directory, could he not enlighten us with definite, specific, and truly detailed knowledge of his time and place— so we get that certain feeling of authenticity that is the next best thing to actual proof?

Assuming for the moment that some very illustrious historical figures chose to manifest through a channeler, would it not be likely that their personality, their character, their style would somehow come through even if translated into the English language so that they might be understood by us?

I recall one of my earliest cases when the late medium and researcher Eileen Garrett accompanied me and the late *Daily News* columnist Danton Walker to his pre-revolutionary house in the Ramapo hills. There Eileen slipped into deep trance and became the vehicle for a badly wounded, suffering soldier of Polish origin who told us his terrible story, haltingly and piecemeal, to be sure, including his name and the people he had been with. The authenticity of this voice was incredible; the name and circumstances also checked out.

More recently, the clairvoyant and trance medium Yolana Lassaw, who often works with police on unsolved crimes, accompanied a detective of the New York Police Department and myself to the site of a grisly murder that had not been solved. In sudden, deep trance, Yolana, who knew absolutely nothing of the case or where we had taken her, spoke with the voice of the actual victim, pointing the finger at one of the suspects on whom the police needed more information to close their case.

On the other side of the coin, a comely lady who makes her living as a competent psychic reader, assured me on a television program we shared that she was the channel for St. Thomas Aquinas. And what did St. Thomas have to say to us mortals? Pretty much the same platitudes you get from most UFO contactees about the Space Brothers who want to save the world from itself. Nothing about theology, deep thoughts, history—this St. Thomas was strictly unreal. But, "I channel his essence," she intoned. Essence? Impersonating a Saint?

Anyone with a gift of turning a clever phrase can claim to be channeling some exotic long ago personality or *Master*. In Jon Klimo's very good book about channeling, the foreword by the eminent psychical researcher Charles T. Tart makes no bones about the evidence (or lack of it), but suggests that the process of dealing with channeled material may help us know ourselves better. Perhaps it does.

Nothing in scientific research is an absolute. Not every Ascended Master is a figment of the imagination. But some kind of evidence should be required before accepting the communication as genuine and as something external to the channeler or medium. Years ago, the late Mrs. Ethel Johnson Myers, one of the finest trance mediums we have had in America, who had worked with me on dozens of hauntings and brought through amazing evidence of a detailed nature, fell into deep trance during one of our many sittings. It so happened that the respected astrologer Charles Jayne was present with us. A personality not at all sounding like Mrs. Myers spoke through her, greeting the astrologer and engaging in an hour's worth of technical conversation about the exact position and orbits of certain planets including the ones not yet discovered in our Solar system, which had been Mr. Jayne's specialty so to speak. After the session was over, Jayne went ahead and verified the material given him by the communicator, who had freely given his name, Kamaraya, and the approximate time of his life on Earth. Even that name is correct for the period and country of origin, something the medium, Mrs. Myers would scarcely have known; her training was in music.

In the end, the proof of the pudding is in the eating: If the seeker wants sugar-coated platitudes, then indeed any channeler will do nicely. If the seeker is truly interested in communicating with an entity of higher intelligence, however, the seeker ought to be more sanguine as to what represents the basic minimum of evidentiality in such communications.

The alleged communicator from the Great Beyond should identify himself in some manner subject to verification, if not by individual name, then by authentic knowledge of the period and place claimed by the communicator. Group sessions are of course more difficult to manage in that respect. Still, the right to question the communicating entity directly should be demanded by those taking part in such sessions and plunking down money for it.

Then the nature of the material coming through the channel itself should be examined critically. Channelers claiming only some vague long-dead Master as their source will have to be questioned when they are "themselves" and not channeling. The differences, if any, in style, knowledge background, delivery of phrases, between the channeler and the alleged communicator must be examined. If the claimed source is someone very well known, this is even easier. Only a very naive and little-educated person should be taken in by such pretenses.

Finally, it is just possible that some of the channeled pseudo-wisdom is helpful to the individuals listening. After all, Dianetics and EST, though widely attacked as highly questionable, may have helped some people over their problems. But the occasional benefits of channeling, in some cases where the material fits a preexisting need that the participant does not want to address in a more conventional manner, should not be misinterpreted as validating the method employed here. True deep trance is a genuine psychic phenomenon, which, in the right hands, can be very helpful both as a scientific tool of inquiry into the nature of man, and a vital link between our world and the next one. The large number of casual channelers are not a part of this link.

The human mind, consciousness working through the physical brain while we are in the physical body, is capable of many things not acceptable to old-fashioned empiric science, but nevertheless true. Tapping deeper levels of one's own consciousness, or that of others, and deriving useful information from such sources, is not only possible, but common. It is neither supernatural nor does it require involving a guru in order to be valid.

The Search for Former Selves

While some, seeking wisdom, will go to a channeler to hear what an ascended master might convey to enlighten them, others are fascinated by who they themselves may have been in some other lifetime—perhaps hoping that in another life they were more interesting or highly evolved than they find themselves in this lifetime. What we are talking about here is, of course, reincarnation—the possibility that we may be reborn into new bodies to gain more experience the next time around—although the term *past lives* has, in recent times, become in vogue.

In the East, the idea of rebirth and cycle of karma are old hat, and readily accepted as part of religious philosophy and orientation. In the West, the study of evidence for reincarnation owes a great deal to the respected parapsychologist, Dr. Ian Stevenson of the University of Virginia, and his initial work, *Twenty Cases Suggestive of Reincarnation*. This watershed work presented strong and convincing evidence that reincarnation was in fact a real phenomenon of human life, that the subject of past lives acquired the aura of scientific possibility and became a subject that could be discussed openly among researchers.

Contrary to lay opinion, these cases have occurred all over the world and not primarily in India, where people believe in reincarnation. But Stevenson took the search out of metaphysics and into the realm of scientific inquiry where it is necessary for evidential standards to be high. Detailed information of a previous existence, including names, dates, places, and circumstances, must be ferreted out for a case to merit attention. If the claimant to a previous life experience is shown to have had no easy access to such information, and if that information turns out to be correct, the case for reincarnation seems strong. Personally, I add still another condition to proof of reincarnation: The claimant should not have any psychic ability, demonstrated either before or after the reincarnation incident or incidents. The reason is that communication by another entity would be an alternate explanation for the material obtained, if it can be shown that the recipient is psychic and has had psychic experiences before. The proof becomes narrower, to be sure, but also stronger in cases where no alternate explanation will suffice.

In the case of Pamela Wollenberg of Illinois, the young lady, then 18, sought me out because of recurrent dreams in which five words were spoken to her by an entity she saw in the dream state. The words were "Ruthven . . . Gowrie . . . Scotland 1600 . . . I leapt." They made no sense to her, nor, for that matter, to me at the time. But subsequently I went to Scotland and started to investigate the matter. With considerable difficulty and diligent search, I finally found confirmation in an obscure book locally published about events in the Highlands. The Ruthven family, whose "second" or noble name was Lord Gowrie, had been wiped out by the king in retaliation of an earlier abduction when he was a lad.

That was precisely in the year 1600, and Gowrie Castle was renamed Huntingtower Castle, to wipe out even the name of the hated family. One of the ladies of the Gowries had apparently been caught in a lover's room by her approaching mother. She ran out and jumped (leapt) from one of the two castle towers to the other, over the roof, and thus successfully escaped her pursuing mother.

How was a simple, 18-year-old upstate Illinois girl to know this? Subsequent investigation through extended hypnotic regression established additional, detailed information, all of which I was able to corroborate later; I published it as probably the best case for reincarnation I had come across. Here we had an "innocent" subject, Pamela, who had neither family background in Scottish history, nor the appropriate education, nor access to the rare book I found in Scotland that gave me the key to the puzzle. Nobody in his right mind would accuse her of making up the story, and for what gain? She was disturbed by all this and came to me for answers, which she did indeed get. True past lives simply do not get recognized in detail in a half-hour session with a reader. At best, a psychic may pick up some foreign elements about the person being read psychically, from the person's own vibrations. It appears that in all of us, without exception, past life elements remain deeply imbedded to develop the personality through each successive incarnation. But these past elements are seldom detailed or even clear. In some cases, bits and pieces of sudden flashes of memory suitable to some person other than the one having them, may emerge, in the déjà vu experience or in recurrent dreams. I have found, over the years, that only unfinished or unsettled lives in the past allow for these bonus memory bits in the present lifetime, perhaps to make this time around a little easier to deal with in compensation for past deprivations.

It is my conviction, based on years of active work in this field, that genuine reincarnation (past lives) memories make themselves known to the person sooner or later by themselves. They can either be ignored, or pursued for clarification. Unquestionably, if one person reincarnates, then we all do. But I have found that only a comparatively few will remember or be able to trace those past lives in a way that is truly and fully convincing. Naturally, it may make a person feel truly special to believe they have spent an earlier existence in so romantic a place as Tibet or ancient Egypt—two favorites, by the way, of past lives readers, along, of course, with the Holy Land at the time of Jesus, but evidence and proof of such people having actually existed is another matter.

Just as with the channeling craze, the proof of authenticity lies in the specifics obtained through past life regression. If a past lives reader who practices his or her craft without benefit of deep regressive hypnosis comes up with substantial information unknown at the time to both subject and reader, well and good—the evidence speaks for itself. But rarely does this happen. Even in professionally induced hypnotic regression, which I have practiced for many years and often (but not always) successfully, the cases yielding specifics capable of verification under the previous restrictive conditions are few. Still, even a few such cases tend to prove the reality of reincarnation.

Some otherwise honorable psychics mistake their ESP abilities for genuine past lives information. They may pick up information about the client from the client's own unconscious, or even an ongoing spirit communication between client and a discarnate entity, and wrongly determine that this outside personality is the client in a previous lifetime. Unless careful research is done and certain test conditions are met, this kind of past life work tends to be more imagination and suggestion than true reality. When an otherwise responsible person lays claim to be the reincarnation of a well-known historical figure, the proof is hard to come by.

The two cases I am about to report have nothing to do with eager past lives practitioners telling their clients within five minutes of meeting them who they were in a previous lifetime. The late General George Patton repeatedly claimed to have been the reincarnation of Julius Caesar and based his conviction, in part, on two elements: his seemingly unwarranted familiarity with the part of France that was Caesar's Gaul during the Roman leader's victorious campaigns there, and an inner voice guiding him in his own campaigns in World War II.

The actor Ernest Borgnine believes he was once "Horatio at the bridge," a legendary Roman hero we know only from Latin classics and, perhaps, tradition, rather than hard historical fact.

Then there is still another category of past lives people sometimes think they experience, even without being told so by anyone—a loved one, who passed on years before, returning as a child or relative. Mrs. Smith in Oregon assured me her young son, age 7, was really her first husband, dead 15 years, come back to be with her. She was sure of it because of certain traits the child possessed.

There are, of course, true cases of reincarnation, nearly all where someone has died prematurely or tragically, returns relatively quickly, and is recognized by someone in this life. Such is the case of a young boy in India, reported by Professor J. Banerjee, who insisted that he had a wife in a distant village. The parents of the youngster eventually gave in and took him to the village he indicated. There, spontaneously, he made for the house he claimed had been his and picked out a middle-aged woman in it, by name, calling her his wife! In the ensuing session the youngster had accurate knowledge of a detailed nature about his alleged previous life to the extent there was no doubt about the truth of his claims. This being India and not America, the parents agreed for the boy to take up residence in the house and with the family of his "former" wife!

During World War II, an American GI was sent to Europe and, with some buddies, was the advance guard in a military detachment entering a village in Belgium where he of course had never been before. They were simply looking for enemy stragglers. But as the three soldiers rounded a street corner, the GI in question made straight for a certain house. "My house, my house!" he cried out, to the puzzlement of his comrades. Quickly, they entered the now empty house and up the stairs to a second floor. At this point, the other two men started to question their comrade about his claim that this was "his house."

Very agitated by now, he assured them it was, and that he had been a child in it, growing up " a long time ago." And to prove his point, he told the others what lay around the bend when they would enter the upper story. He described a painting that would be found there and all the furnishings in the room they had not yet entered. Sure enough, when they did, it was exactly as he had said. Coincidence? Surely not. Clairvoyance, or ESP? Not likely— this GI had never shown the slightest psychic ability or interest before, or after the incident.

◆━━ ㅌ◆ㅌ ━━◆

Mrs. Frank lives in Macon, Georgia, with her husband. On a European trip, the couple, as part of a group tour, found themselves in Florence, Italy, for the first time. Suddenly, Mrs. Frank broke away from the group and insisted on walking through an elaborate iron gate of a palazzo across the street they were on. Nothing could stop her, and, for that matter, Mrs. Frank later described her experience as one of utter compulsion to enter that house at all cost, because she once lived there in another lifetime! Having done so, her emotions becalmed themselves and she returned once more to the others. Apparently there had been the need for her to acknowledge and be aware of her previous existence. The question remains, what made her come to that house, to Florence, in the first place?

When I taped a pilot for a proposed television program in Cleveland a few years ago, a group practicing "suggestive regression" under the control and guidance of a professional esoteric group leader caught my attention, and we proceeded to watch a session. Each of the dozen or so participants, all of them women, by the way, went into a meditative state first, presumably to tap their deeper levels of consciousness including past lives memories. Each in turn then spoke up and told me who they had been before. At least two of the ladies were sure they had been Egyptians, but the young woman who assured me she was Isadora Duncan, the dancer, in a previous life, and the Cleveland housewife who claimed to have been Queen of Sheba, Solomon's lover, particularly interested me. I realized these notions were their harmless fantasies, and knew of at least two other  Isadora Duncans in other cities myself, so I did not even attempt a serious investigation. But what little I saw and heard made it clear to me that these two nice ladies did not know the personalities they claimed to have been in a previous life very well at all.

Anybody who wishes to believe he or she lived before as someone markedly different (and probably more interesting) than their present circumstances is welcome to their dream. However, I feel less charitable when I am confronted by an increasing number of casual practitioners giving past life readings at a price. None of them use professional hypnotic regression to see whether there is, in fact, any memory of a possible previous incarnation, but prefer to do their readings intuitively and generally in terms that are incapable of true verification in books or records of any kind. A particularly crass case dealt with a lady who had been complaining of pains in her wrists and feet; she had not been able to get a medical explanation that satisfied her (such as arthritis, rheumatism, or just tension), but met a young lady who had the right answer. Apparently those pains were due to crucifixion at the time of Jesus! With that, the pains seemed to cease, or at least recede from the patient's attention.

Dr. William Yaney, the eminent psychiatrist of Beverly Hills, California, who includes reincarnation trauma in his treatment of patients, with the help of a good trance medium as his assistant, told one male patient that the terrible pain in his legs was due to his having lost them in another lifetime. The patient accepted the explanation, and learned to live with his problem.

But unless there are specific data, such as names, dates, and places given, the past life material, even when it turns out to be beneficial to the patient, is rarely more than just another psychological trick.

Past lives are sometimes blamed for something done in this life that would otherwise be socially unacceptable. A publisher of esoteric materials and tapes divorced his wife when he met another young lady he fancied immediately. They had been together in another lifetime, and needed to resume in this one.

What, then, is one to do to avoid being taken in by one or another past lives reader, who, incidentally, may well believe fully in their work and its authenticity. There aren't that many conscious frauds among them, but quite a few self-deluded people, and even they occasionally help a client, though not in the way they think. If an honest quest for truth is what you are looking for, certain precautions in dealing with such practitioners are called for.

To begin with, never talk about yourself or what you think you were in a prior life. Don't answer the reader's questions along these lines either. If the reader tells you of an existence in another life, insist on details—when, where, what name. Chances are, the reader will do one of two things: make them up to sound substantial or tell you, "sorry, I don't get those details." Either way, take everything you are told with a big grain of salt.

True, acceptable past life evidence is always possible. But in all the years of my practice in parapsychology, I have found that such material is almost never searched out deliberately in the hope of finding something. Instead, the signs suggesting that regressive hypnosis might have positive results must be present before this ought to be undertaken, and done by a professionally trained person, not a housewife or salesman turned past life reader by her or his own volition.

Some signs of potential past life recall:

- Recurrent dreams (identical dreams keep coming back and are well recalled on awakening).
- Extended déjà vu experiences in a place the percipient has not been before, and that contain particulars regarding the previous connection.
- Knowledge or ability in a field not acquired consciously in this lifetime, such as a strange foreign language, or technical knowledge.
- "Memories" of places and situations one is not familiar with in normal life, and has had no access to through books, newspapers, television, etc.

If you observe these signposts carefully, pursuing the quest for evidence of past lives can be stimulating and truly worthwhile. We all have lived before, but the majority does not have conscious knowledge of it in this lifetime. Those who do, or are able to recall under regression, are nearly always people whose previous lives came to abrupt or violent ends, at least as far as my own records show.

The two subjects—channeling and reincarnation—are not really that closely related. After all, one deals with communications by some spiritual entity eager to use the human channel, and the other with an individual's past lifetime and experience. However, they have one common bond: Both are open to the human frailty known as deception, including, of course, self-delusion.

Past life regression should only be undertaken by a trained hypnotist. The material obtained from the entranced subject should contain names, places, dates, or other data, which can be checked out scientifically from available records or other sources. Names and places that can not be traced may be authentic, but without the confirmation of scientific research. Of course any names or place names of meaning to the subject in his or her normal waking life must be excluded as evidence. Only material not known to the subject can be accepted as evidence.

So the next time a past life reader tells you about some exotic existence in a far away place and time—take her to lunch and tell her she is from even further away; her words are nothing more than thin air.

PART TWO:

The Other Side
of Life

CHAPTER 7

WHAT IT'S LIKE ON THE OTHER SIDE OF LIFE

Our beliefs concerning what happens after we die most often mainly derive from our religious orientation, or perhaps personal philosophy, if *organized religion*, as it is called by those who prefer other ways to express their spiritual attitudes, is not acceptable. Organized religion, the various churches and other communities built around houses of worship, seem similar to business enterprises, with the organizations and all their activities being more of a social order than spiritual.

By and large, all religious faiths have a belief in a supreme deity. That deity is thought to be male, except among Pagan groups, where the deity is called the Mother Goddess.

Since time immemorial we've also held a notion of rising up into what is usually referred to as heaven and the dwelling place of angels, as well as the dear departed, or else being taken down somewhere, usually called hell, sometimes with a purgatory world as a staging area in between. While nobody has been able to pinpoint exactly where these places are, the information derived from departed souls through mediums—psychic individuals—has generally been rejected by people following specific religions or faiths. Such explanations have been seen as dangerous or at least questionable.

The trouble with this attitude, which certainly is the most prevailing one regardless of which faith or religion to which one refers the question, is that the tenets and claims of organized religion are strictly claims and not subject to verification in scientific or realistic terms. Faith, or belief, is what is expected from the faithful, not demands for objective proof. But it is precisely that objective proof, that *evidence* not requiring blind acceptance on faith, that marks the emerging understanding of what really happens to us when we die. When we speak of evidence, we naturally need to know the source of that evidence. Belief or disbelief are to be avoided in the search for real and realistic answers that can and will seriously affect one's view of the "hereafter."

I am not the only parapsychologist accepting this emerging view of what happens to us after we die, but I am certainly in a minority amongst professional psychical researchers who have, for many years, been concentrating on finding all the answers in the living person, thus eliminating the need to accept or even consider the existence of another level of consciousness beyond the physical one.

Professor Joseph Banks Rhine, the father of modern parapsychology and inventor of the term *extrasensory perception* (ESP), spent most of his time and energy researching, and trying to prove that man's spiritual potential rests with the *living* human being as a kind of "special gift," natural, to be sure, and not available to just everybody, but to some select people who have the gift and are developing it by its usage.

In my early years as a researcher, I held that extrasensory perception was not a separate ability possessed by a minority of special people, but an extension of the ordinary five senses beyond what we had assumed to be their limits but were, in fact, not. With this structure I had remained safely within the scientific view of parapsychology of the time. Today, many researchers in the field still cling to this view, which makes other scientists feel more comfortable in respect to the acceptance of parapsychology as being truly scientific.

But in recent years, much of my investigations of this subject has been done with the help of competent and proven trance mediums. Finally arriving at a consensus of what information comes from that multitude of sources, yet matches completely into a single picture, has altered and widened my view of the universe and of what we call our physical life. In addition, I have experienced direct cases involving that wider and truly real world, and accepted the mounting evidence with which these last 10 years have presented me, as the true picture of life beyond death.

There are three parts to our being. The first part, our personality, if you wish, is a kind of electromagnetic field with specific impulses differing with each individual but capable of being measured as to its energy presence.

The second part is an outer, physical body, which dissolves at physical death, because its limited ability to last has expired due to illness or simply because its effective usefulness has expired. This is the body we present to the world; it is certainly mortal in every sense of the word.

But inside that body, and extending slightly beyond it, perhaps a quarter to a third of an inch, is the third part—an exact duplicate body made up of matter too, but much finer matter moving at a higher vibrational rate than the vibration, or movement of the particles that constitute the physical, heavier body. This second body is often called the etheric body or simply the aura and it, too, is an electromagnetic field in its composition. But this duplicate, finer body is what survives death and our persona inside it, moves right on into the surrounding world, just as real and three dimensional to those who live in it, as is the denser physical world for the living.

The only difference is that in place of what we know as time, there is instead a sense of events, and with no physical, mortal body, there is naturally also an absence of illness. Those who go across the divide between our physical world and the spirit world while still sick, especially when they have been full of medications that, while potentially healing to a physical body wreak havoc with an electromagnetic body, will at first be taken to the equivalent of hospitals for cleaning up before being set free to live fully on the Other Side of Life. The world into which we pass when our physical body is dissolved is a world not so different from this one, well organized and well run, where we find our loved ones and others we knew alive and well unless they already have chosen to return here to the physical world through the process of reincarnation. As will be seen in the story of Peggy C., told in the next chapter, everyone on the Other Side has a job, as well.

Will we encounter heaven and hell? Angels and devils? In a word, no. Those concepts are the creation of organized religion and are supposed to be accepted by the faithful. From a scientific standpoint, these are best considered—if one thinks of them at all—in literary terms, because they are, in fact, created fictions. Neither heaven nor hell are objective places, but the Other Side is a beautiful world, even if it reminds one of the world they have just left. It is simply a more pristine, more beautiful version of our world. In it, you will live a full life, do what you like, and meet whom you wish to meet amongst those who have gone over before.

Appearances on the Other Side

Numerous reports from psychic contacts and mediums inform us that once on the Other Side, we may choose for ourselves how we appear to others, most electing to show themselves in their former "prime of life."

William W. lives and works in Washington, D.C. Because of some remarkable psychic incidents in his life, he began to wonder about survival of human personality. One evening he had a dream in which he saw himself walking up a flight of stairs where he was met by a woman whom he immediately recognized as his elderly great-aunt, who had died in 1936:

> "She was dressed in a long, gray dress about the turn of the century style, her hair was black and she looked vibrantly young. I asked her in the dream where the others were, and she referred me to a large room at the top of the stairs. The surroundings were not familiar. I entered the room and was amazed to see about 15 people in various types of dress, both male and female, and all looking like mature adults, somewhere about the age of 30. I was able to recognize nearly all of these people although most I had seen when they were quite old. All appeared jovial and happy."

Communication With the Living

Communication with our physical world is always possible. But it must be initiated by the Other Side, and anyone wishing to communicate with someone here must have a valid reason and get clearance to do so from the guides, who oversee the world we have then passed into. Receiving said permission, one then can communicate with the loved ones left behind. This communication can be direct if the person over there had that gift while in the physical state, but otherwise it must go through a competent medium. Much more will be said about communication between our world and the next in Chapter 9.

Seven Levels

When a person dies, he or she is immediately received into the Other Side, usually by a kind of reception committee of loved ones or friends, who will convey the individual to a first stop, depending upon the individual's character and the circumstances of death.

There are seven levels to the Other Side of Life. Although I would argue that his book's title is a misnomer (*Heaven and Hell*, neither of which, I have just explained, exist), Emanuel Swedenborg, the esteemed Swedish theologian, scientist, and philosopher already knew of and described these levels during the mid-1700s.

Level 1

Level 1 is a very dark world, in which the negative, the guilty, or otherwise disturbed people would land. This level, in the character of its inhabitants, would correlate somewhat to the hell and purgatory of religion. However, there is nothing necessarily eternal about it. From there, an individual will eventually develop to higher levels.

This "hell" is really less picturesque than the one that torments so many who fear it, without brimstone and hell-fires and fellows in red underwear tormenting the sinners. As for sin, there is no such absolute. But there is the absence of good. It is, if anything, a world where the sin of omission (not to do good) is probably the only real sin left.

Level 2

Level 2 is where the vast majority of us ordinary individuals would land, average but good people who have lived average lives.

Level 3

Level 3 belongs to the advanced souls, those who may become guides or teachers and assist people on the physical level when needed. Access from level to level requires guidance and cannot be undertaken at will as the vibrations differ from level to level, becoming increasingly quick as one rises to the higher levels.

Level 4

Level 4 people begin to form groups who work together, for everybody works or has a purpose or assignment over there. There are no harp-playing little girls with goose feathers on their backs.

Level 5

Level 5 is where you will find the avatars, those whose contributions on the physical level have been outstanding and who will now be taught to direct their efforts towards the world at large, always under the guidance of the guides, the teachers, who control communications and assign individuals to specific tasks.

Level 6

Level 6 is where "the government," the administration, sits. There are just nine of these high souls. We might refer to them as angels, but they do not use that term, which means "messenger," for they are not messengers. They call themselves simply "the Beings of Light." The one who is their leader is named Michael. At one time, there was a 10th such being, but that being has left the group. Michael, with whom we had the pleasure of conversing, will not discuss it.

What you have then is a well-organized place, a bureaucracy of sorts, in which there are no exceptions from the divine law, no matter how many prayers you send forth into the ether. Only the Beings of Light can make the decision whether or not your prayer will be answered and how.

Level 7

Level 7 is the highest level, which appears to the Beings of Light only as a huge pulsating light source. This is God—by whichever name you prefer to call this force—the power at the top of the universe. Whether God appears as a source of enormous light or power or is still further behind it, we do not as yet know. But what I report is all I have obtained in my multiple research into the nature of the Other Side of Life.

What I have learned is via a direct link with those who dwell on that Other Side, and it is a multiple read from the material obtained in many sessions. I have no doubt whatever that this is indeed the real picture of what lies beyond our physical deaths.

The absence of some cherished figures of conventional religions does not surprise me in the least. There is nothing about the saints, Jesus, or the other great prophets of all times and religions, from Moses to Mohammed to Buddha and others, perhaps less known but just as powerful in their impact on their people.

This "heaven" is perhaps more heavenly than the one religion calls paradise, and it corresponds to the facts as we now know them. I would suspect that the majority of humanity while believing in God or a god, does not really expect a reception committee once they leave their physical body. But they do get a reception, like it or not. Oblivion, the obliteration of the self—the persona—is not factual. Life is indeed eternal, even though we change from one condition to another. We will have the privilege to choose to stay on the Other Side of Life in a timeless world, or to return for another go at it in the physical world. It is your choice, but the details are up to the people on the Other Side, and depend on what is required for your further development, upwards of course.

CHAPTER 8

NEAR-DEATH EXPERIENCES: PROOF OF A HEREAFTER

While it is true that the evidence for communication with the dead will present the bulk of evidential material for conditions and laws existing in that other world, we have also a number of testimonies from people who have entered the next world without staying in it. The cases involve people who were temporarily separated from their physical reality, without, however, being cut off from it permanently into the state we call death. These are mainly victims of accidents, who recovered; people who had undergone surgery and, during the state of anesthesia, had become separated from their physical bodies and were able to observe from a new vantage point what was being done to them; and, in some instances, people who had traveled to the next world in a kind of dream state and observed conditions there, which they remembered upon returning to the full state of wakefulness. I hesitate to call these cases dreams because the dream state covers a multitude of conditions, some of which, at least, are not actual dreams but states of limited consciousness and receptivity to external inputs. Out-of-body experiences are also frequently classed with dreams while, in fact, they are a form of projection in which the individual is traveling outside the physical body.

The cases I am about to present for the reality of this phenomenon are, to the best of my knowledge, true experiences by average individuals. I have always shied away from accepting material from individuals undergoing psychiatric care, not because I necessarily discount such testimony but because some of my readers might. As Dr. Raymond Moody noted in his work, there is a definite pattern in these near-misses, so to say, the experiences of people who have gone over and then returned.

What they relate about conditions on the Other Side of Life is frequently similar to what other people have said about these conditions, yet the witnesses have no way of knowing of each other's experiences. They have never met and have not read a common source from which they could draw such material if they were in a mood to deceive the investigator, which they certainly are not. In fact, much of this testimony is reluctantly given, out of fear of ridicule, or perhaps because the individual himself is not sure what to make of it. Far from the fanatical fervor of a religious purveyor, the individuals whose cases have been brought to my attention do not wish to convince anyone of anything, but merely to report to me what has occurred in their lives. In publishing these reports, I am making the information available to those who might have had similar experiences and wondered about them.

We should keep in mind that the percipient of the experience would perceive entities and conditions in a three-dimensional way because he himself is three-dimensional in relation to the experience once he leaves his physical body. Thus it is entirely possible that an actual person would appear to the observer exactly the same way as a projection of a person would appear. If we accept the notion that the world beyond this one, in which so-called spirit life continues, is capable of creating by mind actual images of self as desired and even constructing buildings by thought alone, yet is able to make them appear as solid and three-dimensional as people and houses are in this world, then the question of seeming contradictions to physical law as we know it is no longer such a puzzling one. Obviously, an entity controlled by thought can pass through solid walls, or move at instantaneous speed from one place to another; during the temporary states between physical life and death, individuals partake of this ability, and therefore, undergo experiences that might otherwise be termed hallucinations. I cannot emphasize strongly enough that the cases I am reporting in the following pages do not fall into the category of what many doctors like to call hallucinations, mental aberrations, or fantasies. The clarity of the experiences, the full remembrance of it afterwards, the many parallels between individual experiences reported by people in widely scattered areas, and finally the physical conditions of the percipient at the time of the experience all weigh heavily against the dismissal of such experiences as being of hallucinatory origin.

Mrs. Virginia S. is a housewife in one of the western states but has held various responsible jobs in management and business. On March 13, 1960, she underwent surgery for, as she put it, "repair to her muscles." During the operation, she lost so much blood she was clinically dead. Nevertheless, the surgeons managed to bring her back, and she recovered. This is what Mrs. S. experienced during the period when the medical team was unable to detect any sign of life in her:

"I was climbing a rock wall and was standing straight in the air; nothing else was around it, it seemed flat, at the top of this wall was another stone railing about 2 feet high. I grabbed for the edge to pull myself over the wall, and my father, who is deceased, appeared and looked down at me. He said, 'You cannot come up yet. Go back, you have something left to do.' I looked down and started to go down, and the next thing I heard were the words, 'She's coming back.'"

Mrs. J. L. H. is a housewife, in her mid-30s, and lives in British Columbia. She had an amazing experience on her way back from the funeral of her stepfather. Mrs. H. was driving with a friend, Clarence G., and on the way there was a serious accident. Clarence was killed instantly, and Mrs. H. was seriously hurt. "I don't remember anything except seeing car lights coming at me, for I had been sleeping," Mrs. H. explained. "I first remember seeing my stepdad, George, step forward out of a cloudy mist and touch me on my left shoulder. He said, 'Go back, June, it's not yet time.' I woke up with the weight of his hand still on my shoulder."

The curious thing about this case is that both people were in the same accident, yet one of them was evidently marked for death while the other was not. After Mrs. H. recovered from her injuries and returned home, she woke up one night to see a figure at the end of her bed holding out his hand toward her as if wanting her to come with him. When she turned her light on, the figure disappeared, but it always returned when she turned the lights off again. During subsequent appearances, the entity tried to lift Mrs. H. out of her bed, ripping all the covers off her, and forcing her to sleep with the lights on. It would appear that Clarence could not understand why he was on the other side of life while his friend had been spared.

⊷⊶ ⊠⊹⊠ ⊷⊶

Mrs. Phyllis G., who is from Canada, had a most remarkable experience in March, 1949. She had just given birth to twin boys at her own home, and the confinement seemed normal and natural. By late evening, she began to suffer from a very severe headache, however. By morning she was unconscious and was rushed to the hospital with a cerebral hemorrhage. She was unconscious for three days while the doctors were doing their best to save her life. It was during this time that she had a most remarkable experience:

> "My husband's grandmother had died the previous August, but she came to me during my unconscious state, dressed in the whitest white robe, and there was light shining around her. She seemed to me to be in a lovely quiet meadow, her arms were held out to me, and she called my name, 'Phyllis, come with me.' I told her this was not possible, as I had my children to take care of. Again she said, 'Phyllis, come with me, you will love it here.' Once again, I told her it wasn't possible. I said, 'Gran, I can't, I must look after my children.' With this she said, 'I must take someone. I will take Jeffrey.' I didn't object to this, and Gran just faded away. Jeffrey is the first twin that was born."

Mrs. G. recovered, and her son Jeffrey wasn't taken either, and is now 28 years old and doing fine. However, his mother still has this nagging feeling in the back of her mind that perhaps his life may not be as long as it ought to be. During the time when Mrs. G. saw her grandmother, she had been thought clinically dead.

There are many cases on record where a person begins to partake of another dimension, even while there is still hope for recovery, but when the ties between consciousness and body are already beginning to loosen. An interesting case was reported to me by Mrs. J. P. of California.

> *While still a teenager, Mrs. P. had been very ill with influenza, but was just beginning to recover when she had a most unusual experience. One morning her father and mother came into her bedroom to see how she was feeling. "After a few minutes I asked them if they could hear the beautiful music. I still remember that my father looked at my mother and said, 'She's delirious.' I vehemently denied that. Soon they left, but as I glanced out my second floor bedroom window towards the wooded hills I love, I saw a sight that literally took my breath away. There, superimposed on the trees, was a beautiful cathedral type structure from which that beautiful music was emanating. Then I seemed to be looking down on the people. Everyone was singing, but it was the background music that thrilled my soul. A leader dressed in white was leading the singing. The interior of the church seemed strange to me. It was only in later years, after I had attended services in an Episcopal church and also in a Catholic church, that I realized the front of the church I saw was more in their style, with the beautiful altar. The vision faded. Two years later, when I was ill again, the scene and music returned."*

On January 5, 1964, Mr. R. J. I. of Pittsburgh, Pennsylvania, was rushed to the hospital with a bleeding ulcer. On admittance, he received a shot and became unconscious. Attempts were immediately made to stop the bleeding, and finally he was operated on. During the operation, Mr. I. lost 15 pints of blood, suffered convulsions, and reached a fever of 106 degrees. He was as close to death as one could come and was given the last rites of his church. However, during the period of his unconsciousness, he had quite a remarkable experience:

> "On the day my doctor told my wife I had only an hour to live, I saw, while unconscious, a man, with black hair and a white robe with a gold belt, come from behind an altar, look at me, and shake his head. I was taken to a long hall and purple robes were laid out for me. There were many candles lit in this hall."

Many cases of this kind occur when the subject is being prepared for surgery or while undergoing surgery. Sometimes an anesthetic allows dissociation to occur more easily. This is not to say that people hallucinate under the influence of anesthetic drugs, due to the lack of blood, or from any other physical cause. If death is the dissolution of the link between physical body and etheric body, it stands to reason that any loosening of this link is likely to allow the etheric body to move away from its physical shell, although still tied to it either by a visible silver cord, or by some form of invisible tie, which we do not yet fully understand. Otherwise, those who have returned from the great beyond would not have done so.

Mrs. J. M. is a widow in her early 50s, mother of four, and a resident of Canada. She was expecting her fourth child in October of 1956 when she had this experience:

> "Something went wrong, and when I had a contraction, I went unconscious. My doctor was called, and I remember him telling me he couldn't give any anesthetic as he might have to operate. Then I passed out, but I could still hear him talking and myself talking back to him. Then I couldn't hear him any longer, and I found myself on the banks of a river with green grass and white buildings on the other side. I knew if I could get across I'd never be tired again, but there was no bridge, and it was very rough. I looked back and I saw myself lying there with nurses and doctors around me, and Dr. N. had his hand on the back of my neck and he was calling me and he looked so worried that I knew I had to go back. I had the baby, and then I

was back in the room, and the doctor explained to my
husband what happened. I asked him why he had his hand
on my neck, and he replied that it was the only place on
my body where he could find a pulse, and for over a minute
he couldn't even feel one there. Was this the time when I
was standing on the riverbank?"

Deborah B. is a young lady, living in California, with a long record of psychic experiences. At times, when she's intensely involved in an emotional situation, she undergoes what we parapsychologists call a dissociation of personality. For a moment, she is able to look into another dimension and partake of visionary experiences not seen or felt by others in her vicinity. One such incident occurred to Deborah during a theater arts class at school, when she looked up from her script:

"I saw a man standing there in a flowing white robe, star-
ing at me, with golden or blond hair, down to his shoul-
ders; a misty fog surrounded him. I couldn't make out his
face, but I knew he was staring at me. During this time I
had a very peaceful and secure feeling. He then faded
away."

Later that year, after an emotional dispute between Deborah and her mother, another visionary experience took place:

"I saw a woman dressed in a long, blue, flowing robe with
a white shawl or veil over her head, beckoning to a group
of three or four women dressed in rose colored robes
and white veils. The lady in blue was on the steps of a
church or temple with very large pillars. Then it faded
out."

One might argue that Deborah's imagination was creating visionary scenes within her, if it weren't for the fact that what she describes has been described by others, especially people who have found themselves on the threshold of death and returned. The beckoning figure in the flowing robe has been reported by many, sometimes identified as Jesus, sometimes simply as a Master. The identification of the figure depends, of course, on the religious or metaphysical attitude of the subject. But the feeling caused by his appearance seems to be universally the same—a sense of peace and complete contentment.

Frequently, people undergoing near-death experiences report floating through a brightly lit tunnel, where they encounter dead relatives or friends. There they see a light at the end of the tunnel—but just before they reach it, there is an authority figure, or sometimes a dead relative telling them to "go back, it is not your time," and back they go, waking up in their beds.

Mrs. C. B., of Connecticut, has had a heart problem for more than 25 years. The condition is under control, as long as she takes the tablets prescribed for her by her physician. Whenever her blood pressure passes the 200 mark, she reaches for them. When her pulse rate does not respond to the medication, she asks to be taken to the hospital for further treatment. These drugs are injected into her intravenously, a procedure which is unpleasant and which she tries to avoid at all costs. But she has lived with this condition for a long time and knows what she must do to survive.

On one occasion she had been reading in bed and was still awake around 5:00 in the morning. Her heart had been acting up again for an hour or so. She even applied pressure to the various pressure points she knew, in the hope that her home remedies would slow down her pulse rate, but to no avail. Because she did not wish to wake her husband, she was waiting to see whether the condition would abate by itself. At that moment, Mrs. B. had a most remarkable experience:

> "Into my window flew or glided a woman. She was large, beautiful, and clothed in a multicolored garment with either arms or wings close to her sides. She stopped and hovered at the foot of my bed, to the right, and simply stayed there. I was so shocked, and yet I knew that I was seeing her as a physical being. She turned neither to the right nor to the left but remained absolutely stone-faced and said not a word. Then I seemed to become aware of four cherubs playing around and in front of her. Yet I sensed, somehow, that these were seen with my mind's eye rather than with the material

eyes. I don't know how to explain from any reasonable standpoint what I said or did, I only knew what happened. I thought, 'This is the angel of death. My time has come.' I said audibly, 'If you are from God, I will go with you.' As I reached out my hand to her, she simply vanished in midair. Needless to say, the cherubs vanished too. I was stunned, but my heartbeat had returned to normal."

Mrs. L. L. of Michigan dreamt, in July of 1968, that she and her husband had been killed in an automobile accident. In November of that year, the feeling that death was all around her became stronger. Around the middle of the month, the feeling was so overwhelming she telephoned her husband who was then on a hunting trip, and informed him of her death fears. She discussed her apprehensions with a neighbor, but nothing helped allay her fears.

On December 17, Mrs. L. had still another dream, again about imminent death. In this dream she knew that her husband would die and that she could not save him, no matter what she did. Two days later, Mrs. L. and her husband were indeed in an automobile accident. He was killed and Mrs. L. nearly died. According to the attending physician, she should have been a dead woman, considering her injuries. But during the stay in the hospital, when she had been given up on, and was visited by her sister, she spoke freely about a place she was seeing and the dead relatives with whom she was in contact at the time. She knew that her husband was dead, but she also knew that her time had not come—that she had a purpose to achieve in life and therefore could not stay on the plane on which she was temporarily.

The sister, who did not understand any of this, asked whether Mrs. L. had seen God, and whether she had visited heaven. The unconscious subject replied that she had not seen God, nor was she in heaven, but on a certain plane of existence. The sister thought that all of this was nonsense and that perhaps her dying sister was delirious.

Mrs. L. remembers quite clearly how life returned to her after her visit to the other plane. "I felt life coming to my body, from the tip of my toes to the tip of my head. I knew I couldn't die. Something came back into my body, I think it was my soul. I was at complete peace about everything and could not grieve about the death of my husband. I had complete forgiveness for the man who hit us, I felt no bitterness toward him at all."

Do some people get an advance glimpse at their own demise? It would be easy to dismiss some of the precognitive or seemingly precognitive dreams as anxiety-caused, perhaps due to fantasies of their own. However, many of these dreams parallel each other and differ from ordinary anxiety dreams in their intensity and the fact that they are being remembered so very clearly upon awakening.

A good case in point is a vivid dream reported to me recently by Mrs. Peggy C. who lives in a New York suburb. The reason for her contacting me was the fact that she had developed a heart condition recently and was wondering whether a dream she had had 20 years before was an indication that her life was nearing its end. The dream that so unnerved her through the years, had her walking past a theater where she met a dead brother-in-law:

> *"I said to him, 'Hi Charlie, what are you doing here?' He just smiled, and then in my dream, it dawned on me the dead come for the living. I said to him, 'Did you come for me?' He said, 'Yes.' I said to him, 'Did I die?' He said, 'Yes.' I said, 'I wasn't sick. Was it my heart?' He nodded, and I said, 'I'm scared.' He said, 'There is nothing to be scared of, just hold onto me.'*
>
> *"I put my arms around him and we sailed through the air in darkness. It was not a frightening feeling but a pleasant sensation. I could see the buildings beneath us. Then we came to a room where a woman was at a desk. In the room was my brother-in-law, an old lady, and a mailman. She called me to her desk. I said, 'Do we have to work here too?' She said, 'We are all assigned to duties. What is your name?' I was christened Bernadine but my mother never used the name. I was called Peggy. I told her 'Peggy.' She said, 'No, your name is Bernadine.'*
>
> *"After taking the details, my brother-in-law took me by the arms, and was taking me upstairs, when I awakened.*

I saw my husband standing over me with his eyes wide open, but I could not move. I was thinking to myself, 'Please shake me, I'm alive,' but I could not move or talk. After a few minutes, my body jerked in bed, and I opened my eyes and began to cry."

The question is, did Mrs. C. have a near-death experience and return from it, or was her dream truly precognitive, indicative perhaps of things yet to come?

Dr. Karlis Osis has published his findings concerning many death-bed experiences, wherein the dying recognize dead relatives in the room, seemingly come to help them across the threshold into the next world. A lady in South Carolina, Mrs. N. C., reported one particularly interesting case to me recently. She has a fair degree of mediumship, which is a factor in her case:

"I stood behind my mother as she lay dying at the age of some 70 years. She had suffered a cerebral stroke, and, at this particular time of her life, she was unable to speak. Her attendants claimed they had had no communication with her for over a week previously. As I let my mind go into her, she spoke clearly and flawlessly. 'If only you could see how beautiful and perfect it all is,' she said, then called out to her dead father, saying 'Papa, Papa.' I then spoke directly to her and asked her did she see Papa? She answered as if she had come home, so to speak. 'Yes, I see Papa.' She passed over to the Other Side shortly, in a matter of days. It was as if her father had indeed come after her as I had spoken with her when she saw him and spoke clearly with paralyzed mouth and throat muscles."

Sometimes the dead want the living to know how wonderful their newly found world is. Whether this is out of a desire to make up for ignorance in one's Earth life, when such knowledge was either outside one's ken or ignored, or whether this is in order to acquaint the surviving relative with what lay ahead. Cases involving such excursions into the next world tend to confirm the near-death experiences of those who have gone into it on their own, propelled by accidents or unusual states of consciousness.

One of the most remarkable reports of this kind comes to me through the kindness of two sisters, living in England. Mrs. Doreen B. is a senior nursing administrator who has witnessed death on numerous occasions. Here is her report:

"In May, 1968, my dear mother died. I had nursed her at home, during which time we had become extremely close. My mother was a quiet, shy woman, who always wished to remain in the background. Her last weeks were ones of agony; she had terminal cancer with growths in many parts of her body. Towards the end of her life, I had to heavily sedate her to alleviate the pain. After saying good-bye to my daughter on the morning of the seventh May, she lapsed into semiconsciousness and finally died in a coma, approximately 2:15 a.m. on the eighth May, 1968.

"A few nights after her death, I was gently awakened. I opened my eyes and saw Mother. Before I relate what happened, I should like to say that I dream vividly every night, and this fact made me more aware that I was not dreaming. I had not taken any drinks or drugs, although, of course, my mind and emotions revolved around my mother. After Mother woke me, I arose from my bed, and my hand instinctively reached out for my dressing gown, but I do not remember putting it on. Mother said that she would take me to where she was. I reacted by saying that I would get the car out, but she said that I would not need it.

"We traveled quickly, I do not know how, but I was aware that we were in the Durking Leatherhead area and entering another dimension. The first thing I saw was a large archway. I knew I had seen it before, although it means nothing to me now. Inside the entrance a beautiful sight met my eyes. There was glorious parkland, with shrubbery and flowers of many colors. We traveled across the parkland and came to a low-built white building. It appeared to be a convalescence home. There was a veranda, but no

windows or doors as we know them. Inside everything was white, and Mother showed me a bed, which she said was hers. I was aware of other people, but they were only shadowy white figures. However, I was aware that one of a group of three was a man. Mother was very worried about some of them and told me that they did not know that they were dead.

"*Mother had always been very frugal in dress, possibly due to her hardships in earlier years. Therefore her wardrobe was small but neat, and she spent very little on clothing if she could alter and mend. Because of this, I was surprised when she now expressed a wish that she had more clothes. In life, Mother was the kindest of women, never saying or thinking ill of anyone, therefore I found it hard to understand her resentment toward a woman in a long flowing robe, who appeared on a bridge in the grounds. The bridge looked beautiful but Mother never took me near it.*

"*I now had to return, but to my question, 'Are you happy?' I was extremely distressed to know that she did not want to leave her family. Before Mother left me, she said a gentle 'Good-bye dear.' It was said with a quiet finality and I knew that I would never see her again.*

"*It was only afterwards, when I related it to my sister, that I realized that Mother had been much more youthful than when she died and that her back, which in life had rounded, was straight. Also I realized that we had not spoken through our lips but as if by thought, except when she said, 'Good-bye dear.' It is now three and a half years since this happening, and I have had no further experience. I now realize that I must have seen Mother during her transition period when she was still earthbound, possibly from the effects of the drugs I administered under medical supervision, and when her tie to her family, particularly her grandchild, was still very strong.*"

Patricia N., sister to Mrs. B., kindly wrote her own account of the incident, "separately and without consulting each other." As Mrs. N.

remembers it, her sister reported the incident to her shortly after it occurred:

> "My sister told me that she felt herself being gently shaken awake and when she opened her eyes, my mother was bending over her. She was wearing ordinary dress and looked as she did some 25 years earlier."

Mrs. N. then goes on to confirm pretty much what her sister had written to me. She adds:

> "She told my sister she would not be staying where she was but gave no indication as to where she was going. There were no other buildings to be seen in this vast parkland area. It otherwise appeared to be totally deserted and exceptionally beautiful and peaceful. My deepest regret is that my sister and I had never taken an interest in ESP, spiritualism, or mediums up to that time and were therefore totally unprepared for what happened."

Sometimes the dying want their family to know of their passing immediately rather than wait to make contact later, when they reach the Other Side. Don McIntosh is a professional astrologer living in Richland, Washington. He has no particular interest in psychic phenomena, is in his early 70s, and worked most of his life as a security patrolman, his last employment being at an atomic plant in Washington state. After retirement, he took up astrology full-time. Nevertheless, he had a remarkable experience that convinced him of the reality of afterlife existence.

> "On November 15, 1971, at about 6:30 a.m., I was beginning to awake, when I clearly saw the face of my cousin beside and near the foot of my bed. He said, 'Don, I have died.' Then his face disappeared, but the voice was definitely his own distinctive voice. As far as I knew at that time, he was alive and well. The thought of telling my wife made me feel uncomfortable, so I did not tell her of the incident. At 11 a.m., about four and a half hours after my psychic experience, my mail arrived. In the mail was a letter from my cousin's widow, informing us that he had

had a heart failure and was pronounced dead upon ar-
rival. She stated that his death occurred at 9:30 p.m.,
November 8, 1971, in Ventura, California. My home, where
my psychic experience took place, is at least 1,000 miles
from Ventura, California. The incident is the only psychic
experience I've ever had."

There are repeated reports indicating that the dead, because they are able to project a thought-form of themselves as they wish, revert to their best years, which lie around the age of 30 in most cases. On the other hand, where apparitions of the dead are intended to prove survival of an individual, they usually appear as they looked prior to death, frequently wearing the clothes they wore at the time of their passing.

The number of cases involving near death experiences—reports from people who were clinically dead for varying lengths of time and who then recovered and remembered what they experienced while unconscious—is considerable. If we assume that universal law covers all contingencies, there should be no exceptions to it. Why then are some people allowed to glimpse that which lies ahead for them in the next dimension, without actually entering that dimension at the time of the experience? After investigating large numbers of such cases, I can only surmise that there are two reasons. First of all, there must be a degree of self-determination involved, allowing the subject to go forward to the next dimension or return to the body. As a matter of fact, in many cases, though not in all, the person is being given that choice and elects to return to Earth. Secondly, by disseminating these witnesses' reports among those in the physical world, knowledge is put at our disposal, or rather at the disposal of those who wish to listen. It is a little like a congressional leak: short of an official announcement, and much more than a mere rumor. In the final analysis, those who are ready to understand the nature of life will derive benefits from this information, and those who are not ready, will not.

I think, fortunately, fear of telling about NDEs may be diminishing with the increased attention this phenomenon has received in recent years. A New Jersey physician, Dr. Joseph Guzik, recently admitted publicly that he had died after a severe attack of pneumonia in 1934 and could actually see himself lying on his death bed. At that time, he worried what his mother would say if he had died, when he heard a voice tell him that it was entirely up to him whether he wanted to stay on the physical plane or go across. Because of his own experience, Dr. Guzik now pays serious attention to the accounts of patients who have similar experiences. Not all NDEs involve the journey through the tunnel or the arrival on the Other Side at the opposite end, but many do.

CHAPTER 9

GHOSTS, SPIRITS, AND HAUNTINGS

Ever since the successful, fictional motion picture *Ghost* (1990) stirred the imagination and curiosity of millions of people all over the world, the question of ties beyond physical death has become a subject one can seriously discuss, even in groups who would have laughed at such possibilities a scant dozen years ago. So perhaps the field of parapsychology owes Hollywood at least this debt.

Western society has been brainwashed for centuries by organized religion to let well enough alone, give unto the world what concerns your body, and give unto the church what concerns your soul, or whatever it is you become when you die. People in some Eastern countries are less hostile to the notion of a tangible, real hereafter, though not necessarily because of scientific reasons. Religion, all of it, assumes there is another world waiting when you leave this one, but it looks askance on any attempt by us directly, to find out what it is like. Leaving that intelligence-gathering and interpretation to the clergy is rarely very helpful. At best it will give a partisan glimpse at that next dimension into we all must pass. At worst, a distorted, even frightening view of what lies ahead.

The truth of the matter is that we already have so much hard evidence, from scientifically valid sources, regarding the next state of existence, that one need not live one's life in ignorance and fear.

Love on the Other Side

To understand how love and romance, yes, and sex, can exist between people in the physical world and those who once were, but are no longer in it, one should first come to understand the very nature of life itself. Only then does continuing communication and continuing bonds with those on the Other Side of Life make sense. In the final analysis, the nature of deep emotional relationships within the framework of the existing universe we know, will then also become clearer. It does not mean we will, or can, have all the answers, but we will be able, by examining our true nature, to deal with such incidents properly—neither with fear nor with fanatic passion, but naturally, as each and every situation requires.

When one partner passes out of the physical world, the other partner, left behind, will grieve, and eventually, get over it, often finding another romantic mate. That is as it should be, though grieving for someone who has gone on is not helpful to either the one who grieves or to the one grieved for, as it will affect them adversely. Most often, attentions from the dead lover are not encouraged from a living partner.

An elderly Canadian lady had divorced her husband long before he died, but immediately after he passed over, he started contacting her and making every effort to continue what he still perceived as a relationship. She did not want it. She had not wanted it before he died and wanted it even less afterwards, but he persisted and caused her much anguish, until we were able to break his hold on her psyche at least to the extent she was able to control his incursions.

When people pass over to the Other Side, nothing in their character changes immediately: Unfulfilled desires are as strong as before. They will try to get back to their usual surroundings, their old homes, and impress their companion with their presence. Depending on the degree of the living person's psychic abilities, it will work well, badly, or not at all. But such attempts are rarely frightening or dangerous to the living.

Roseanne Schaffer is a very attractive, self-assured woman who makes her living in several ways. Using the name Fahrusha, which means butterfly, she does Eastern dancing. She also is a very busy tarot reader and psychic consultant, appearing all over the country at fairs, colleges, and clubs.

Because her father was psychic, the subject was never disbelieved in her home as she grew up; her father was a marine engineer, but mediums, psychics, and séances were always part of their lives in Union City, New Jersey.

When she was only a precocious 14, Roseanne caught the eye of a young man a few years older than herself. Dennis was 18 when they met at a Masonic convention; the bond was there instantly, and they began to date. They saw each other for several years, and a romantic bond developed between them, even though a physical relationship did not, due to her young age.

When Roseanne was in a school play, Dennis came to rehearsal to see her. When she saw his silhouette entering the auditorium, something very strange occurred.

Suddenly Roseanne felt herself transported back in time, wearing old-fashioned clothes and having the appearance of a woman of about 24–28. A young man came down what appeared to be a walkway in New England, looking about age 30 or thereabouts, and they met and embraced with a feeling of incredible joy. Twenty seconds later, she was back in real time, still 15 years old, and the stranger was just Dennis. Had this been a flashback to an earlier lifetime she and Dennis had shared?

Dennis worked for the railroad as a brakeman. One day there was a terrible accident: Dennis was crushed between cars, and died at the hospital shortly after.

At that time, Roseanne had not seen him for several months, and only saw his obituary later. By then she was in college, dating another man. At the time Dennis died, in November 1973, she had been 18, Dennis, 22.

But shortly after Roseanne had become aware of his death, she experienced a strange sensation in the early mornings. It felt like a "waking dream," in which she could not wake up even though she was fully aware of her surroundings. Then there was a tingling sensation all over her face and neck, as if she were being touched by something electric.

It dawned on her that someone was trying to get in touch with her. The dreams began to come more often, and it was always Dennis and herself having a nice time, going out, enjoying each other's company—and yet she heard herself say, in the dreams, "but you are dead!" Once or twice, she heard her name called softly, just "Rose . . ." and the tingling of her face and neck felt indeed like kisses—kisses from the Beyond.

Roseanne is not upset by all this, even though Dennis is still "hanging around" to this very day. She is too busy with her career to worry.

To be sure, the majority of physical encounters between a discarnate and a living person are not exactly welcome or, for that matter, ideal in any sense. That is not to say that such relationships are not tangible in certain ways (such as the "kisses" experienced by Roseanne), and not just in the fertile imagination of the living partner!

There are also some cases where the incursion from Beyond is not exactly sought, but encouraged through prayer, meditation, strong feelings of loneliness, and a desire to have the physical relationship somehow continue.

But what I am about to report is none of the previous. The parties involved did not know each other, or of each other, until they shared the same physical space.

I thought I had "laid to rest" a certain young lady ghost in a Brooklyn College residence, but lo and behold, the story was apparently not quite finished. Some time after my initial investigation, when I followed up on a report by four girls who lived in an apartment in that house, I was contacted by some male students in great excitement: "Henny," as they had come to call the ghost, was apparently still active, and would I please do something about it?

Henny used to live in one of those old brownstone houses in a better section of Brooklyn. The house had been turned into a boarding house for students and professional people. Henny worked in a department store, having been unable to finish college. But she always had a great admiration for those who did, and dated many students, and even teachers, over the years. Dated is perhaps the wrong term, because Henny had both an extremely good figure, and an insatiable appetite for sex. Unfortunately, she also had a heart defect and passed away in her 30s. What had been her room at the boarding house was used by many others as time went on.

I don't know whether people had problems with her ghost before the time I heard about it, but a couple of Brooklyn College students called me in great excitement when Henny appeared to them.

> *George, one of the two young fellows, had gone to bed in his room in that house, when he was awakened late in the night by a strange glow emanating from the ceiling. He checked it out and found no source for it, but decided to blame passing cars. He had hardly laid down again, when the glow became brighter and turned into the pulsating figure of a young woman, dressed in clothes of another era.*

> *George sat up in bed and watched dumbfounded as the woman came toward him and began to stroke his head. He actually felt her caress, though it seemed very cold and clammy when her hands touched his forehead.*

> *Being half awake, George somehow thought that she was one of the girls from the upper floors who was putting on a trick for him, but he really did not mind. Especially as the girl also took off her blouse and pressed her breasts against his chest. He could not help observing that her breasts were enormous and that her lips, touching his, were cold as ice.*

George does not remember any more than this: When he awoke the next day, he thought it had all been a sexy dream. I made light of it to his landlady, who was not at all amused by his graphic description of the girl's assets. "You wait here a moment," she finally demanded and rushed off to her own apartment. When she returned a moment later, she held a yellowed newspaper clipping in her hand. "Does that look anything like the woman you saw in your dream?" she asked. George took a look at the clipping. "Why, it is her," he replied. The clipping was the girl's obituary from more than 20 years ago!

Because I had been asked to do something about poor Henny, I returned a week later with a good trance medium, Mrs. Ethel Johnson Meyers, and we contacted Henny. The contact broke her obsession with the living, and she left, somewhat tearfully, but in peace.

When a close relationship of a romantic or sexual kind (or both together) comes to an end because one of the two participants passes out of the physical world, the continuance of that relationship is usually impossible for obvious reasons. But there are a number of instances where the obvious difficulties are being overcome by the sheer passion and life force of the dead partner, proving once again that life, by no means, ends at death's door.

For the surviving lover, this represents problems that need to be addressed. If attentions from beyond the grave are welcomed, or even actively encouraged, they will of course preempt any new relationship on the physical Earth level. The choice is ours. If the continuing romantic or sexual incursions of the dead partner continue and are not welcome because a new relationship has been formed by the surviving half, then there is need to deal with it in an appropriate way.

Obviously the partner in the spirit dimension will hear and see the partner in the physical world, and if the surviving partner will address the other lover in a kind, but firm manner to express the desire to discontinue the attempts at a relationship from the Beyond, chances are the other person will abide by their wishes, for no one wants to stay where he or she is not wanted. But then again, there are cases where this will not do, if the dead lover is so hung up on the physical relationship that he or she will not listen to the living partner's plea.

In the extreme case, where it becomes a serious threat to a new relationship, an exorcism is in order. An exorcism is not by any means a fanciful discourse by a learned clergyman with a supposed devil (a figment of the Church's imagination), but a ritual request to let go of the entanglement and to go on to the next state of existence in peace and with love. I have conducted such rituals, usually successfully, and both parties found peace afterwards, in their own way, in their own world.

It is unwise, in any event, to allow a relationship to continue between people living in two different worlds, no matter how close they may have been before one of them passed over. On the other hand, a continuing friendship and love, other than romantically possessive and exclusive, is not necessarily evil or even undesirable. In time, the partner who has passed on will be reconciled to the separation, or perhaps even return through the process of reincarnation, which affects all of us in different ways, at different times, as is suitable to each and every individual. The guides who control such contacts do not approve of them, however, and do not give their permission. But the force may be so strong as to overcome their refusal.

In the final analysis, if we are to accept a greater scheme of things than what our rational mind can grasp, we will also accept the separation of death between lovers as part of that scheme, painful though it may be to us as individuals.

But it is wise to keep in mind that a continuing love or active physical relationship between a discarnate and an incarnate person holds back the development of the soul of both parties in their respective lives. Remember, too, that the world into which all of us will eventually pass, is not so far away, nor so terribly different from this one, and that *life never ends*.

Ghosts and Stay-Behinds

No other aspect of the paranormal has been so little understood, by large segments of the population, as experiences with apparitions or auditory phenomena suggesting a presence from beyond.

To begin with, *ghosts* are in a state between the two worlds—the physical world we live in, and "the world next door" as Eileen Garrett, the famed medium, put it. Roughly the equivalent of what religion likes to call purgatory (but without the sinister implications of punishment), it is a state that requires adjustment. Ghosts are in it because of unfinished business in the physical state, sudden death not understood, trauma at the time of passing, or shock—in short, emotional turmoil which, most of the time, prevents them from realizing what to do about it.

Ghosts are almost never harmful in any way, the two lone exceptions coming to mind being the case of a murder in the Philippines after which the perpetrator returned to the place of his crime, and was done in by his then-dead victim, and that of an insane medieval bishop of Trondhejm, Norway, who liked to push visitors to his church down from the gallery. But it is safe to assume that a ghostly apparition (or voice) cannot even help itself, much less harm you.

Ghosts, however, are the exception to the rules of passing over. Most of us, at the time of death, simply leave our outer, physical body and glide into the etheric or spiritual dimension that already surrounds us—the main difference being that now we inhabit a duplicate body, with all our senses and memories fully intact. Moreover, because the next world occupies the same wavelength as the wavelength of our etheric inner bodies (which has now become our *only* body), we are as solid in that world as we were in our outer, heavier body in the world we've just left. When a spirit contacts someone in the denser, physical world, it moves through solid objects with seeming ease, just as polaroid light can penetrate other light without difficulty, while occupying the same space.

There is still a major difference between what we commonly call ghosts and free spirits: Ghosts are firmly held in place at or near the spot of their passing, by their emotional ties and unresolved issues. Free spirits, all of those who are not ghosts, come and go as they wish, though I have long ago learned, through numerous contacts and much research, that even free spirits need permission from a regulator to make contact with people in the physical world. These regulators are called spirit guides; religiously oriented people like to call them angels, though they are ordinary people like you and me, who have passed over to the Other Side and have been given certain assignments in accordance with their abilities and desires, that is, their jobs. Nobody goofs off on the Other Side!

It should, however, also be understood that all ghosts are not created equal, so to speak. To begin with, a vast portion, perhaps as much as two-thirds of all sightings (and ghostly voices) are, in fact, only impressions from past events, which a sensitive person can easily pick up. They are not people, but are more like a television picture or radio broadcast frozen in time that has long been separated from the ones involved.

It is not easy to distinguish, at times, which is which. Probably the best way is to determine whether exactly the same sighting, at the same time, has been observed by different witnesses. Real ghosts vary their performances—their appearances—just as physical people do.

Finally, there is the notion that ghosts are always the result of a terrible event, and are trying to overcome their pain, which in their minds has never ended. In many cases this may indeed be so, but not in others, where less fearsome events caused the person to fall into the in-between state of a ghost. Either way, the approach in relieving them is the same for the experienced parapsychologist.

But there are many cases where an individual who has been living for a very long time in a house dies and has never been told about the Afterlife or does not believe it exists. Such people simply stay put when their physical bodies are done with, and keep going through the same motions as they were used to in life.

They are free spirits, yet they can't leave, or won't leave, because they don't know where to go. But they are aware of a change in their condition, are rational (which ghosts are not), and are sometimes more difficult to dislodge and send on to their dimension than emotionally disturbed ghosts—simply because they feel they have a right to stay in *their* houses! For them, I have created the term *stay-behinds*.

Generally, these are people who have lived with some form of formal religion in their lives, fully expecting to go to heaven, with all the trimmings (or in some cases, perhaps, fearful of going to "the other place," which they really believe exists!) and now find that very little has changed. Oh, they know they are dead, of course, they know full well that a funeral has taken place, but they don't feel any different than before, except perhaps that their aches and pains are now gone.

So they are neither poor souls suffering in an in-between state or from unfinished business, nor free spirits en route to the Other Side, but something in between: the stay-behinds.

Sounds and a Number of Sightings

Outside of Boston, in a trailer park at Peabody, Massachusetts, lives a lovely lady of Austrian descent by the name of Rita Atlanta (not her real name, but the name under which she dances in nightclubs). Rita came to America at an early age after undergoing some horrifying experiences at the hand of occupying Russian troops in her native Austria.

She became a well-known dancer in nightclubs both in this country and in Europe and it was in Frankfurt, Germany, where we first met. At that time she had read one of my books and had explained to me that she needed some advice concerning a ghostly apparition in her trailer. It seems unusual to hear about ghosts in a trailer park, but I have heard of ghosts in airplanes and in modern apartment buildings—not all ghosts flit about old Victorian homes—so I was not particularly surprised.

We spent about an hour talking about Miss Atlanta's other ESP incidents, of which she had had a number over the years, and looked at her album of show business photographs. Rita told me that whenever she did not travel on business, she and her teenage son lived in a trailer outside Boston. Sometimes they spent months at a time there when things were slow in the nightclub business. The boy went to school nearby, and was looked after by his grandmother.

The trailer itself is fairly large and looks no different from any other of the same type, situated on its own foundation. The sides are made of metal and inside the trailer there is a large bedroom, a dining room, a kitchen, and a small room, almost the same as a conventional small apartment. Miss Atlanta was upset by the goings-on in her trailer:

Night after night, at 3:00 in the morning, she would wake from deep sleep to see a man, wearing a dark overcoat, standing in front of her bed and staring at her. She could not make out his face, nor could she see his feet, yet there was no mistaking the tall figure of a man coming out of nowhere without the benefit of doors opening and clearly for reasons of his own.

It did not frighten Rita, for she had had psychic experiences before. But she began to wonder why this stranger kept appearing to her in what she knew was a new trailer, having bought it herself a few years prior. Even her son saw the stranger on one occasion, so she knew that it was not her active imagination causing her to see things.

She began to ask questions of neighbors, people living in other trailers in the park. Finally she came upon an assistant to the manager of the camp who had been there for a long time. He nodded seriously when she described what was occurring in her home. Then he showed her a spot on the road just in front of her trailer, explaining the cause of her problem: Some years before, a man roughly fitting the description she had given had been run over and killed by a car. Clearly the apparition was the restless spirit of the man who had died in front of her trailer; he was confused as to his true status. Whenever his spirit recalled the moment of his untimely death, he apparently had felt a compulsion to look for help and the nearest place to look would have been her trailer. Ever since Rita and I discussed this over coffee in her trailer, the apparition has not returned.

The 1780 House, so named because of the large date 1780 over the door, just beneath the American eagle, is one of the finer Colonial houses in the Stamford, Connecticut, area. At the time of this story, Mr. Robert Cowan, an advertising executive, and his wife Dorothy, both of whom had an open mind about such things as ghosts, owned and lived in it.

The house has three levels. In what today might be called ground level or even cellar, the Cowans used the large room next to the kitchen for their dining room. On the next level was a living room and a kind of sitting room. Beyond that, a corridor led to the master bedroom and den. Upstairs were two guest rooms and a small attic, accessible only through a hole in the ceiling. The house had been built during the American Revolution, standing on a wooded slope and was originally called the Woodpecker Ridge Farm. The Cowans had been in the house nearly 10 years. As soon as we had settled ourselves in front of one of the comfortable fireplaces I asked Mr. Cowan to recount his experiences in the old house.

"From time to time (once a week or so) during most of the time we've lived here I have noticed unidentifiable movements out of the corner of my eye—day or night. Most often, I've noticed this while sitting in our parlor, and what I see moving seems to be in the living room. At other times, and only late at night when I am the only one awake, I hear beautiful but unidentified music seemingly played by a full orchestra, as though a radio were on in another part of the house.

"The only place I recall hearing this is in an upstairs bedroom, just after I'd gone to bed. Once I actually got up, opened the bedroom door to ascertain if it was perhaps music from a radio accidentally left on, but it wasn't.

"Finally, quite often, I've heard a variety of knocks and crashes that do not have any logical source within the structural setup of the house. A very loud smash occurred two weeks ago. You'd have thought a door had fallen off its hinges upstairs, but, as usual, there was nothing out of order.

"My wife had two very vivid experiences about five years ago. One was in the kitchen, or rather outside of a kitchen window. She was standing at the sink in the evening and happened to glance out the window when she saw a face glaring in at her. It was a dark face, perhaps Native American; it was very hateful and fierce.

"At first she thought it was her own distorted reflection in the glass but in looking closer, it was a face glaring directly at her. All she could make out was a face, and as she recalls it, it seemed translucent.

"Then, on a summer afternoon my wife was taking a nap in a back bedroom and was between being awake and being asleep when she heard the sounds of men's voices and of working on the grounds—rakes, and garden tools—right outside the window. She tried to arouse herself to see who they could be, but she couldn't get up."

As the quietness of the countryside slowly settled over us, I could indeed distinguish faraway, indistinct musical sounds, as if someone were playing a radio underwater or at great distance. A check revealed no nearby house or parked car whose radio could be responsible for the sounds.

After a while, we got up and looked about the room itself. We were standing about quietly admiring the furniture, when both my then wife Catherine and I, and of course the Cowans, clearly heard footsteps overhead. We decided to assemble upstairs in the smaller room next to the one in which we had heard the steps. The reason was that Mrs. Cowan had experienced a most unusual phenomenon in that particular room.

"It was like lightning, " she said, "a bright light suddenly come and gone."

I looked the room over carefully. The windows were arranged in such a manner that a reflection from passing cars was out of the question. Both windows, far apart and on different walls, led into the dark countryside away from the only road.

Catherine and I sat down on the couch, and the Cowans took chairs. We sat quietly for perhaps 20 minutes, without lights except a small amount of light filtering in from the stairwell. It was very dark, certainly dark enough for sleep, and there was not light enough to write by.

As I was gazing towards the back wall of the little room and wondering about the footsteps I had just heard so clearly, I saw a blinding flash of light, white light, in the corner facing me. It came on and disappeared very quickly, so quickly in fact that my wife, whose head had been turned in another direction at the moment, missed it. But Dorothy Cowan saw it and exclaimed, "There it is again. Exactly as I saw it."

Despite its brevity I was able to observe that the light cast a shadow on the opposite wall, so it could not very well have been an hallucination. I decided it would be best to bring Mrs. Ethel Johnson Meyers to the house, and we went back to New York soon after.

Actually, two visits with Mrs. Meyers were necessary to clarify the situation. The story was this: A young girl by the name of Lucy, born in 1756, had been in love with a young man named Benjamin. Her grandfather Samuel had killed Benjamin by throwing him down a well in back of the house in 1774. The name Harmon was mentioned. The young man allegedly was buried on the hill and the grandfather was buried to the west of a white structure on the same grounds. The tombstone was broken off at the top. This, according to the medium, was done by vandals.

Not long after these facts were received by Mrs. Meyers, the Stamford, Connecticut Historical Society and some of their volunteer student helpers were given permission to dig around the historical house and grounds. Picture everyone's surprise when they came up with a tombstone with the name Samuel on it, broken off at the top.

The noises heard are common in hauntings, representing energy. The lights seen are the spirits who are encountered—also typical in hauntings.

On the corner of Tenth Street and Second Avenue in New York City stands a church known as St. Mark's-in-the-Bowery. St. Mark's, a Dutch Reformed church, is among the most famous landmarks in New York. It was built in 1799 on the site of an earlier chapel going way back to Peter Stuyvesant, who was governor of New York in the year 1660.

As a matter of fact, Governor Stuyvesant, who became the legendary Father Knickerbocker, is buried in the crypt. The last member of his family died in 1953 and then the crypt was sealed. One can see the crypts from across the street because they are half underground and half above ground, making the churchyard of St. Mark's-in-the-Bowery a unique sight.

The church itself suffered a fire in the 1970s, allegedly due to a cigarette left by a negligent worker during the steeple restorations. Whether the fire was of natural origin or in some way connected with the paranormal goings-on in the church is debatable, but as soon as the charred remains of the roof had been removed, rebuilding on St.-Mark's-in-the-Bowery got started and today it is again what it was before the fire. It is built along neoclassical lines; around the church and the cemetery is a cast iron fence and the church is open most of the time.

St. Mark's boasts of three known ghosts. First there is a woman parishioner who has been observed by a number of reputable witnesses in the middle of the nave, staring at the altar. She has been described as a Victorian woman, very pale, and apparently unhappy. Who she is, nobody seems to know.

Another ghost has been observed on the balcony close to the magnificent organ. Several organists have had the uncanny feeling of being observed by someone they could not see. One of the men working in the church reported hearing footsteps coming up to the organ loft. He assumed that the organist had come to work early and got ready to welcome him when to his surprise the footsteps stopped and total silence befell the organ loft. Needless to say, he did not see any organist.

Finally, there are those who have heard the sounds of a man walking distinctly with a cane and it is thought that the limping ghost is none other than Peter Stuyvesant himself, who, as we know, had a wooden leg and used a cane. His body, after all, lies in the crypt beneath the church.

On Bayberry Road in Somerton, Pennsylvania, not far from Philadelphia, stands a charming little house built in 1732. I visited at the behest of the Robinsons, who had called on me to do something about a Colonial soldier who thought their home was still his place.

Set back somewhat from the road, the house has three floors, and the Robinsons had furnished it with a keen sense of period style. Perhaps that, more than anything else, contributed to the Colonial ghost's presence, as he must have felt very much at home in the place.

Mrs. Robinson is Irish and was no stranger to psychic experiences: When she was but 14, reading in bed one night, the door opened and there stood her brother Paul, which caused her to duck under the covers inasmuch as Paul had been dead for eight years.

> *When the Robinsons moved into the old house, they soon realized they weren't exactly alone in it. Both heard footsteps when no one was walking about, doors would open by themselves, and cold air blasts would be felt without apparent reason. At first, she thought her children were playing pranks but she found out this was not so, the children being fast asleep in their respective beds.*
>
> *It got so that someone unseen would open the door for her, as if to accommodate her. One way or another, the doors would simply not stay shut. A rocking chair would start up by itself. A week before our visit, a rotisserie rack came sailing down the stairs toward her, and had she not ducked quickly, it would have hit her. Clearly, our coming was not viewed enthusiastically by the ghost.*

My first visit had convinced me that a trance medium was required to make contact with this ghost, so when I returned a second time, I had with me the late, famed, British medium Sybil Leek.

As soon as Sybil had relaxed sufficiently, she went into a state of deep trance and the ghost was able to communicate with me through her. It turned out his name was John Ross and the house had been a meeting place, in 1744. Fact is, the house was a Quaker "meeting house," according to records I checked later.

And why Captain John Ross was hanging out in this house, I wanted to know. He confided, through Sybil, that he was all for peace, and that he served in the 25th cavalry regiment. He spoke of a battle in this spot and of having been hurt. He was waiting for "them" to fetch him, but he liked the house because it was "a meeting place to pray." It appears the man, himself a Quaker, was lost, having been killed in battle. Later, I was able to trace John Ross in the Regimental records of the time. Some of the fellow officers he named during the trance also proved to have served during that period.

⊷ ⊷ ⥤◊⥢ ⊶ ⊶

The well-known stage and screen actress June Havoc, until recently, owned a town house in New York City, which stood in a very old part of town. Located at 428 West 44th Street, just west of Ninth Avenue, this impressive Victorian townhouse was built more than 100 years ago and was originally the property of the Rodenberg family. It has four stories and, at the time when it was built, was considered one of the most elegant houses in the area. The area, once a less than desirable neighborhood, and therefore dubbed "Hell's Kitchen," is presently experiencing a vibrant revival—even, some would say, gentrification.

Eventually the house fell into disrepair but was restored to its original appearance both inside and outside by an architect in the 1950s. June Havoc acquired it in 1962 and rented the upper floors to various tenants but kept the downstairs apartment for herself. One reaches Miss Havoc's former apartment by a staircase up to the parlor floor. For some unknown reason, tenants never stayed very long in that apartment, but Miss Havoc paid no attention to that at the time she moved in.

Before long, however, she noticed a number of things. There were strange tapping noises at various times of day and night, and eventually they kept her from sleeping or concentrating on her work. This became particularly loud around 3 a.m.

At first she tried to find a logical explanation for the noises by calling in all sorts of workmen and experts to see whether the house was settling or whether there was something wrong with the piping or the structure of the house. None of these things turned out to be the case. When the noises became unbearable, Miss Havoc called upon me to help her rid the house of whatever was causing the disturbances.

I paid the house two visits, accompanied by Sybil Leek. On the first occasion we also had the company of several distinguished observers, including newspaper columnist Earl Wilson and publicist Gail Benedict. As soon as Ms. Leek had slipped into a trance state, during which her own personality was temporary absent while the alleged ghost was invited to speak through her, it became apparent that something very dramatic had taken place in the house.

A young woman ghost, calling herself Lucy, manifested through the medium, crying out in pain of hunger and demanding food. During my questioning, it appeared that "Hungry Lucy," as I later called her, had lived and died on the spot where the house now stands. Her death had been due, according to her own testimony, to a fever epidemic. She claimed to have lived in the year 1792.

I then asked to know why Lucy was still in the house, what she was looking for. She explained she was waiting for her boyfriend, a soldier by the name of Alfred. Because it is possible to check into the regiments of soldiers, even several hundred years ago, I asked what regiment her Alfred served in. Without hesitation Lucy replied, "Napier." The following day, we checked this out and discovered that Colonel Napier was the commanding officer of a regiment stationed in the grounds of Governor Clinton's estate. The land on which Miss Havoc's house stands was part of that estate in 1792. Further, we found that a fever epidemic had, in fact, occurred at that time, and Colonel Napier had been shipped back to England because of illness. During the séance, we convinced Lucy that there was no point in waiting around for her soldier any longer, and eventually she let go of her compulsion to stay on in the house. Soon she was slipping away and I left Miss Havoc's apartment in the hope that all would be quiet from then on.

However, this was not to be the case. It appears that while we had freed Lucy from the house, we had done nothing about Alfred, her boyfriend who had also died in the area. A second visit was arranged, during which Sybil Leek went into deep trance again. This time, additional contacts were made with men who had lived and died in the area during the Revolutionary period, and we were able to establish that these people had actually existed from comparing their names with entries in regimental and other historical records.

We also addressed Alfred, imploring him to let go because his Lucy was now on the Other Side of Life, and no longer among the living. Ideally, we should have done this at the same time we dispatched Lucy to her just rewards. Unfortunately, though the séance was otherwise successful, Alfred failed to understand us, and the noises continued sporadically. In 1969, Ms. Havoc sold the house and with it relinquished her tenants of the downstairs apartment. But I hear from people living in the house that, now and again, Alfred is still around.

Tom Morgan Jones had been a captain in the Air Force when he and Nancy, an attractive blonde, met and fell in love in her native Little Rock, Arkansas. After three years, Tom decided he wanted to leave his career as a pilot and settle down on a farm. The Joneses returned to Tom's home town of Vineland, New Jersey, where Tom got a job as the supervisor of a large food-processing company.

Tom and Nancy moved into an old farmhouse near Vineland in the summer of 1975. The house had been built in 1906 by a family named Hauser, who had owned it for many generations. Tom's father had acquired it from the last Hauser 19 years before.

Sitting back a few hundred yards from the road, the house has three stories and a delicate turn of the century charm. There is a porch running the width of the front, and ample rooms for a growing family. Originally there were 32 acres to the surrounding farm, but Tom and Nancy decided they needed only four acres to do their limited farming. Even though the house was very run down and would need a lot of repair work, the couple liked the quiet seclusion and decided to buy it from Tom's father and restore it to its former glory.

"The first time I walked into this house I felt something horrible had happened in it," Mrs. Jones explained to me. Yet by the time the family had moved in, Nancy had forgotten her initial apprehension about the house. However, about four weeks later, the first mysterious incident occurred.

As Nancy explained it, "I was alone in the house with my two children whom I had just put to bed. Suddenly I heard the sound of children laughing outside. I ran outside to look but didn't see anyone. I ran quickly back upstairs but my kids were safely in their beds, sound asleep, exactly where I'd left them."

That summer Nancy heard the sound of children laughing several times, always when her own were fast asleep. Then one day, Nancy discovered her daughter Leslie Ann, then age 3 1/2, engaged in lively conversation with an unseen friend. When asked what the friend looked like, the child seemed amazed her mother couldn't see her playmate herself.

Convinced they had ghostly manifestations in the house, they decided to hold a séance with the help of a friend. After the séance, the phenomenon of the unseen children ceased but something else happened:

"We found the gravestone when we cleared the land," Tom said. "We had to move it periodically to get it out of the way. We finally left it in the field about a hundred yards away from the house. Suddenly the day after our séance, it just decided to relocate itself right outside our back door. It seemed impossible—it would have taken four strong men to move that stone."

For some time, Nancy had the uncanny feeling that Ella Hauser, the woman who had built the house was "checking" on the new occupants. Tom Jones had looked on the ghostly goings-on in a rather detached, clinical way, but when his tools started disappearing, it was too much, even for him.

The Joneses were not the only ones who encountered the unknown in the old Hauser farmhouse. In August of 1977, a babysitter, Miss Frame, was putting the children to bed when she heard someone going through the drawers downstairs. "She thought it was a prowler looking for something," Nancy explained, "but when she finally went downstairs, nothing had been touched."

The night after the babysitter incident, Nancy went downstairs to get a drink of water and found a 5-foot 10-inch tall man standing in her living room—at 3:00 in the morning.

"He was wearing one of those khaki farmer's shirts and a pair of brown work pants. Everything was too big for the guy. I could tell he was an old man. I took one look and ran upstairs."

When I received their telephone call, I immediately asked for additional details. It became clear to me that this was a classic case of haunting where structural changes, new owners, and new routines have upset someone who lived in the house and somehow remained in the atmosphere. As is my custom, I assembled the Joneses, and a psychic I had brought with me into an informal circle in the kitchen. Together we asked Ella and whoever else might be "around" to please go away in peace and with our compassion—to enter those realms where they would be on their own. The atmosphere in the kitchen, which had felt rather heavy until now, seemed to lift. When I talked to Nancy Jones several weeks after my visit, all was well at the house.

—◦— ⇒◦⇐ —◦—

One of the oldest and historically most interesting sections of New York City is Greenwich Village, where many houses dating back to the early 19th, 18th, and even 17th centuries still exist. The people living in them sometimes have to share their apartments with an unseen entity, or even a seen one. But ghosts and old houses seem to go together, and those among the people living in this part of New York, whom I have interviewed over the years, have never seemed to think there was anything remarkably horrible about them. If anything, they were curious about the person or persons with whom they shared their homes.

Some years ago, I had the pleasure of meeting a certain Miss Boyd down on Charles Street, and the meeting was mutually useful. Miss Boyd, of course, was a ghost. All of this happened because Barrie, a friend, had taken an apartment at 39 Charles Street, and found that his ground floor apartment contained a ghost. On Halloween, 1964, I visited the apartment in the company of Sybil Leek. I had no idea whom I might meet there, apart from the flesh and blood people then occupying the apartment. There was a fire in the fireplace and an appropriate wind howling outside, but it was novelist Elizabeth Byrd, Barrie's friend, who set the proper mood.

She explained that one of Barrie's house guests, Adriana, had been awakened in bed by a rather violent push on her arm. At the same time, she felt herself compelled to burst into tears and wept profusely, although there was no reason for it. Somehow she partook of another person's feelings, involving a great deal of sorrow. This happened several nights in a row. However, Adriana did not tell Barrie about it. There was no need because one night he arrived around 1:00 in the morning to find Adriana practically drowning in her tears. When his guest left, he tried to dismiss the whole thing, but he, too, felt a presence watching him all the time. On one occasion, he saw a whitish mist, and was sure that someone was looking at him.

Ms. Leek felt communication with the unseen entity was possible. Gradually falling deeper and deeper into a trance state, she made contact with the unhappy woman who could not leave the spot of much suffering in her own lifetime. "Her name is Boyd," Sybil explained, and then the entity, the ghost, took over Sybil's speech mechanism, and I was able to question her about her grievances.

Apparently Miss Boyd was looking for a document having to do with ownership of the house; the year was 1866. The owner of the house was someone named Anussi, or so it sounded to us. At that point, we had to end the séance. We returned, though, a few weeks later, and again Sybil Leek made contact with the ghost. I was fascinated to learn that Elizabeth Byrd had meanwhile done some research on the house and discovered that it had indeed belonged to a family named Boyd ever since it had been bought by one Samuel Boyd in 1827. Even the landlord, whose name we had heard as "Anussi," may have had some basis in fact, except that the name was spelled, "Moeslin."

According to the records, this man had rented the house to Mary Boyd in 1886. But what about the paper the ghost was trying to recover, the paper that apparently caused her continued presence in the house? "Find the paper, find the paper. This is my house," the ghost had said through the medium. The paper, it appeared, was in the name of her father, Bill, and the landlord did not have any right to the house, according to the ghost—that was the reason for her continued presence in the house.

I tried to explain that much time had gone by, and that the matter was no longer of importance. I asked Miss Boyd to let go of the house and join her equally dead relatives on the Other Side of Life. There was no doubt that medium Sybil Leek had indeed brought through an authentic ghost, because Elizabeth Byrd in discussing her research had mentioned only the name Mary Boyd. But in trance, the ghost speaking through the medium had identified herself proudly as Mary Elizabeth Boyd. When the records were rechecked, it was discovered that the person living in the house in 1868 was Mary E. Boyd. There was a William Boyd, evidently the father the ghost had referred to, who had given her the paper proving her ownership and rights to the house.

A Note on Something That Is Not

One common misconception regarding hauntings and ghosts is that there is something different called a *poltergeist*. But poltergeist, meaning "noisy ghost," is only the part of a haunting involving noise or physical movements. It is *not* a different category, but an integral part of nearly all ghostly manifestations.

PART THREE:

Those Creatures

CHAPTER 10

VAMPIRES, DEMONS, AND SUCH

Paranormal research is the thrust of parapsychology, an established and recognized science dealing with phenomena that are scientifically observed and reported and are in no way subject to religious belief or unproven fantasy. Unfortunately, in the minds of many people not really familiar with the fundamentals of this field, the events or experiences dealt with by parapsychology, and the world populated by demons, vampires, and such are one and the same. In fact, the existence of such things are strongly rooted in folklore and religious beliefs, do not belong to serious scientific inquiry, and are totally unconnected with paranormal research.

Of Bats and Blood

I turned on my television to see that one of the talk shows was featuring a lady in the Midwest, who confessed that she enjoyed drinking a little blood now and then. Nothing really dangerous, mind you, and besides, she only bites people she knows really well. She assures the interviewer she considers herself a Vampire.

In Elmhurst, Long Island, you can find the American Vampire Society in the living room of one "Dr." Stephan Kaplan, the world's most famous (and probably only) authority on vampirism. Prior to discovering the lore—and lure—of vampires, Mr. Kaplan was into haunted houses, though I could not accommodate him while investigating the infamous Amityville House for one of my books. (Even earlier in his searching career, Kaplan was in sales.)

Vampires are definitely "in." Francis Ford Coppola's latest version of the Bram Stoker 19th-century novel *Dracula*, was released in December 1992. It didn't matter that some audiences laughed in the wrong places. The kids ate it up. Some pretty good actors played it as if they really believed it. But nobody is ever really, really, scared at such movies. People were far more terrified at an earlier, eerie version by German director Werner Herzog, starring Klaus Kinski, who looks threatening—even without special makeup.

In reality, vampires are actually small bats, at home in the forests (principally in the Carpathian Mountains of Eastern Europe), who fly at night and do like to bite even smaller animals in order to eat them. They do not like biting people and they do not suck blood. But they do look kind of mysterious and scary.

Lots of regular, full-size bats populate old buildings, particularly with towers or belfries. And what could be more desirable to a bat than those dilapidated castles of Hungary and Rumania? I have watched them fly around the stairwell of an Austrian 18th-century chateau at dusk, screeching their peculiar chant, just as an aged lady, who happened to have been a hunchback, came hobbling down the stairs. Hitchcock could not have staged it better.

This sort of thing inspired Brahm Stoker—the English talent agent-turned-novelist—to create his *Dracula*, combining the atmospheric world of bat-infested castles with a real-life medieval tyrant, Vlad the Impaler, Prince of Moldavia (which is now a part of Rumania). The historical Vlad was a mad tyrant who killed his enemies in one of the more bizarre fashions current in the Middle Ages all over Europe—impalement on a sharpened stake—but he definitely was not a vampire. In fact, he died a reasonably normal death: One of his enemies killed him, and good riddance!

The folk tradition of the "undead" is universal, not just Rumanian. It stems from the notion that somehow you can get cheap and willing labor for the fields by nearly killing some people, then reviving them with permanent brain damage, but able to work . . . the Haitian zombies.

In Hungary, Transylvania, and Rumania, peasants always feared the mysterious bat, not being zoologists, and assumed that the strange creatures had something to do with the supernatural, and hence evil. Anything the ordinary folk feared might keep them in line and home at night, the church reasoned, so the mythical vampire assumed anti-Christian and devilish character. That being the case, only the sight of a cross and a Christian prayer would keep the evil one in check.

If a permanent solution was required, one would have to open the vampire's grave—in the daytime of course, when he would be asleep (as bats are)—and, before you can say "Nosferatu," put a wooden stake through his heart. Then, just to be on the safe side, cut off his head. That way, the vampire wouldn't bother anyone any longer, because vampires, according to folklore, must suck blood from people to survive. Moreover, those bitten become vampires themselves—an interesting suggestion, because being scratched or accidentally bitten by a real bat can result in serious infections: bats are disease carriers.

In modern times, vampires survive in the term *vamp*, meaning a seductress, but the notion of a dual existence—good and evil, represented by the vampire myth and character, and also by the equally fictional Dr. Jekyll and Mr. Hyde—are nothing more than creative fictional forerunners of modern psychology. Dr. Freud and the id, and all the jargon of psychoanalysis, have sought to show that dual personalities can indeed exist in one person—but these personalities are, alas, natural, not supernatural in the least.

Demonology

Another matter of considerable concern to some fundamentalist believers is the existence of demons, even though the word itself (*daemon*) is just Greek for "spirit." Belief in demons as the coworkers of the devil has developed from the 13th century onward in Christian theology, since the devil, as the supposed counterplayer to Christ, was first popularized in an effort to head off the widespread survival and popularity of ancient Pagan beliefs and rites among the country folk.

There are those who would like to raise the fiction of demons to a lifestyle, following the path of *demonology*. Such individuals appeal to the demons of nature to come down in "fair and not frightening" appearance and to do their bidding. The belief that this may be possible is very colorful indeed, resting mainly on a classic on the subject, called the *Lemegaton*, now resting peacefully in the British Museum. Taken symbolically, of course, the realm of demons exists in the community of minds that accepts their existence.

It is moot to question the effects of invoking a friendly demon, such as Vasago—the latest center of attention by the reputable group O.T.A. (Order of the Temple of Astarte). In the realm of demons, every force in nature has a demon representing it, and by invoking it, the worshipper hopes to get the help and energy of that particular demon on his or her side. Then there are the demons connected with hell. Of course these demonic beings don't exist either, in the concrete sense, but the term has served some religions well to keep the faithful in line—just as the notion of sin has done.

There is no demonic possession requiring a religious exorcism— except, of course, in films—but there is a very real case to be made for actual possession of living people by *discarnates*, those who have died and desire to express themselves further by taking over a living person. The possessing spirits are psychotic or evil individuals, but they are neither devils or demons, nor do they have any kind of supernatural powers other than their ability to alter a living person's character and behavior. Possession is dealt with by a scientific form of exorcism, working on both the invading entity and the host person who allowed it to occur. But more about this can be found in Chapter 11.

Don't get me wrong, ghosts and spirits—the "dead" who live on in another world—are very real and so is communication with that word; the occasional possession is a malevolent and invasive form of that communication. But "demons" are not real.

As for werewolves—also grist for the mills of horror picture producers—it is true that violent character and personality changes in people can elicit wild, beast-like behavior, but normally these individuals don't grow fur or fangs. Although I even know of a case where a man was actually attacked by a wolf in a way that made him think he was dealing with a human-turned-wolf, there is nothing whatever to this notion either.

Fortunately, the overwhelming majority of moviegoers and readers of books know that vampires, demons, and werewolves are fictional characters and quite harmless to them. Only when someone tries to pretend that they really exist today, in order to frighten people or influence them, do they become a real problem.

To people who don't really know much about valid research into parapsychology, it all sounds the same—ghosts, spirits, ESP, monsters of this or that type, Bigfoot, vampires—just a lot of nonsense without any truth to it. But of course that is not so. Modern parapsychology contains three words it prefers not to use: *belief*, *disbelief*, and *supernatural*. The latter is used in this book only to call it what the uninitiated would call it. In the context of this work, today's "supernatural" is really tomorrow's "natural."

There are a couple of aficionados who like to "investigate" ghosts and hauntings (and demonic invasions), and even run an interesting museum in their home "documenting" demons and demonic matters. In my opinion, it is needless to say that this is all fictional, but they have, in some cases, intervened in genuine hauntings and "poltergeist" cases, delaying the correct approach that could have resolved such cases more quickly along proper parapsychological lines. The couple have attracted quite a bit of publicity: She is a professional psychic— a reader—and he is an artist by profession. They used to have a defrocked priest and former police officer in their train at one time, but I do not know whether that is still the case.

In their visit (unasked) to the well-known house in Amityville, Long Island, where the DeFeo murders took place, they "found" demonic influences. Having been to that house twice myself, with competent mediums and a psychic photographer, the story is now pretty well known: An ancient Indian burial ground was disturbed, setting a chief on the warpath against those in the house, as the land is sacred to the chief and his people. No demons are involved here.

A recent case in point was a "classical case" of a haunted house in rural Pennsylvania, bothered by the well-known and usual "poltergeist" manifestations of objects moving and voices being heard. Literally thousands of such cases have been carefully investigated by professional scientifically trained parapsychologists and often result in a proper "rescue circle," by which the trapped, earthbound spirit in the house is persuaded to leave, and in releasing the spirit, the living are also freed. Unfortunately, teams of self-styled "demonologists" sometimes meddle in such cases, and, far from solving them and bringing relief, frighten the victims with devilish tales of resident demons, until the people in the house flee the manifestations, which could have been dealt with quickly and properly with the right approach.

PART FOUR:

Powers and Possessions

CHAPTER 11

POSSESSION AND EXORCISM

From time immemorial, humans have been fascinated with the possibility of being controlled by some outside force—or of some outside force being able to control them! Much fear surrounds the notion of these possibilities, particularly the latter, but what is known by the general public on the subject is full of misconceptions, and then there is also the problem of outright fallacy and fraud.

The Possessed

Possession is a real phenomenon. It occurs when a discarnate human being inhabits a living person and makes that person behave in a manner contrary to, or markedly different from, that person's normal behavior.

I am familiar with some cases because my services were required, when the individual in question was being treated as schizophrenic. That, unfortunately, is the verdict the average medical doctor will generally arrive at, and the result is that a false diagnosis will lead to improper treatment. Only a trained, academic para-psychologist can distinguish between genuine schizophrenic illness and possession, and nearly all doctors will not even consider the possibility of possession as a diagnosis. Fortunately there are *few*

medical doctors who had training in parapsychology as well and can resolve such cases.

One of these cases involved a prominent publisher's wife, who had been the victim of possession while idly playing with a Ouija board while on vacation with friends. She was not aware of her own mediumship, which opened the door to an entity who was able to take over. The possessing entity was an artist who was also a murderer. At first, nobody would believe her when she described this man being present, but after she was thrown down the stairs and injured, her husband became convinced.

Exorcising the Spirit

The publisher, finally realizing the truth of his wife's condition, called in John Myers, the English medium. Myers tried to dislodge the alien entity, but failed. Finally the joint efforts of Dr. Robert Laidlow, head of the psychiatric department at Roosevelt Hospital, and myself succeeded in dislodging the entity from the body of the unfortunate lady. But in this case, success was short-lived; the possessor had not yet given up. Because the woman was addicted to drinking, he found another entry door, and in the end she wound up a "vegetable" at an institution.

I also was asked to help with the case of a young woman in Boston, who was possessed, according to medium Eileen Garret, who could see the entity clinging to the girl. Fortunately, this case was resolved more positively.

That a hospital would open its facilities for a case of possession is rare indeed, but it happened in Milledgeville, Georgia. A woman who had contacted me from the Midwest, with a plea for help with an unwanted spirit entity that was clinging to her, came to meet me in Georgia, where she had found a sympathetic ear at the local hospital. I came to Milledgeville and, with the assistance of the hospital staff, used deep hypnosis to free the woman of the possessing entity.

In none of these cases is there any hint of anything or anyone diabolic or supernatural. Peter Blatty's successful novel, *The Exorcist*, was based on a true incident that occurred in the Midwest. The phenomena portrayed in the film version (such as the victim's head spinning round 360 degrees, or the victim spewing green bilge) simply did not occur.

The suggestion that it is necessary to use a priest as the exorcist makes a scientifically valid exercise into a religious battle with a demonic force. Exorcism performed by the Church is no more valid than performed by a trained parapsychologist, without the burden of religious trappings. The Church does have such a ritual, but will not perform it unless and until several "experts" (priests) have declared the need—because the possession is genuine, and from their point of view, demonic. The only instance in which a priest's intervention may be more successful than that of a trained parapsychologist's is one in which the possessing entity itself may have been "religious" and will more readily obey a priest-exorcist's urgings to release the victim.

Curses and Spells

What exactly is a curse? Strangely enough, the power of curses is exactly the same as that of blessings. The ancient terms of "malediction" and "benediction" bear witness to the close similarity of the effort involved. It is, of course, true that the negative is more powerful than the positive because it involves, at times, great amounts of hatred within the individual performing the magic act called cursing. To summon similarly strong emotional impacts when blessing an individual is rarely possible.

One of the leading researchers in this area of the occult, Karl Spiesberger, has pointed out that curses are very real things. Curses represent thoughts. Thoughts cannot only create action by their very existence, but are, in fact, also generating thought forms, which he calls *psychogones*.

The basic theory behind the effectiveness of curses is fairly simple. When a person formulates a certain phrase containing strong emotional expressions of hatred, that person is, in actuality, creating thought forms that are both tangible and indestructible. The thought form, imbued with the destructive purpose of the curse, is then sent out either generally or specifically towards one or more individuals. It is not necessary for the receiver of the curse to be aware of it. Because the thought form is in itself a tangible thing, it is effective regardless of the receiver's attitude or position.

In a séance setting, a curse will operate somewhat along the lines of dangerous radiation. When a radioactive agent sends forth radioactive emanations, those radioactive particles reach individual human beings and cause certain reactions, frequently damaging. Radioactivity coats objects as well as people and frequently remains in the atmosphere for long periods of time. By the same token, curses simply do not die away but fade very gradually, both electromagnetically, when the energy created is dissipated over great stretches of time, and emotionally, when the original purpose of the curse has been fulfilled.

Curses, however, differ greatly from impersonal radiation, in that the basic component of motivation of the curse is effective only if the person uttering the curse is truly motivated by strong emotional feelings—generally great hatred, despair, or anger. Curses uttered in jest or without true conviction are completely powerless and ineffective. That is why any empty phrases containing words like "I'll be damned" or "damn you" are of no significance and do not contain any dangers.

When certain religions proscribe the use of the name of the deity in vain, they do not do so because there might be actual damage to the one using God's name without good reason, but purely on dogmatic grounds. Invoking the deity without cause is in violation of proper religious procedure.

Words by themselves are the framework of thought forms. They can differ greatly in their effectiveness, according to the mood in which they are uttered. They are potentially a highly powerful source of electromagnetic energy. That temporarily very strong energy reservoir is condensed by the cursing person into a comparatively small number of words that, in turn, create the thought forms sent forth towards the one for whom the curse is destined. Thus, by compressing a very large psychic force into a very small "container," that container—the curse—becomes very powerful indeed. Spiesberger and other psychic researchers have shown, by citing valid examples, that curses are far from figments of the imagination. They are, in fact, very real energy sources that must be reckoned with.

Not only effective when directed towards human beings, curses also can touch animals or even inanimate objects. They can be directed towards entire towns or lands. Although it seems, perhaps, unbelievable, it is nonetheless true that curses have been found to be so lastingly effective that they have been capable of harming *generations* of people— including many innocent descendants of the original wrongdoers.

The Three Types of Curse

There are two basic groups of curses. A malediction may be formulated to include a general group as its target, or it can be exactly tailored to one individual whom the curser wishes to reach. In the case of a general curse, anyone coming into contact with the broad target, be it a group of persons—such as a clan or family—or a place, will be affected by it. In some cases, general curses are merely intended as protection against unauthorized interference, such as curses that were routinely invoked to protect the Egyptian royal tombs. In the case of a curse toward a specific individual, naturally, the danger is limited to that person.

But there is a third group of curses, which is even more powerful than the other two. That is when the one originating the curse is not satisfied with drawing the utmost of his own energies of hatred and anger from the depth of his self and formulating them into words, but invokes the "powers of darkness" as well to support him in his negative quest. This, of course, is done by following certain ritual magical formulas and can be understood or undertaken only by those well versed in the black arts. By combining his own forces with outside energies derived from the psychic world around him, the magician then forges a "thunderbolt" of hatred that is both extremely effective and difficult to discover. It is even more difficult to counteract.

Nevertheless, there are boundaries beyond which even the most potent curse cannot go. To begin with, any curse reaching its objective and having done what it was meant to do will, of itself, collapse into nothingness. For example, if a curse is uttered against a certain family to strike down that family in all its male members, then upon the death of the last heir the curse will disappear.

But beyond this there is the law of karma, which is superior to any curse. If a curse would interfere with the proper karma of an individual, then the curse would be altered or made ineffective. Simply put, if no misdeed has been performed, yet a curse is uttered against an innocent individual, then that curse will not work. The karmic law requires that every deed be compensated for by another deed. No one need be afraid of being cursed if his conscience is clear. Conversely, if an evil deed has been perpetrated and the perpetrator been cursed, he has every reason to expect the curse to be effective. That, too, is part of the basic karmic law of retribution.

In those cases where the receiver of the curse is made aware of it, and wishes to blunt its effectiveness, he has another avenue open. By expressing pure love towards the one who has cursed him, a man can at least influence the effectiveness of the curse. The more love is poured out towards the perpetrator of the curse, the more likely it is to become ineffective. By the same token, if knowledge of an existing curse leads to great anxiety or even an attempt to run away from the curse, this will only add to the potency of the curse.

On the surface at least, the result of a successful curse seems to be within the natural law and could, seemingly, be explained by a chain of misfortunes not necessarily connected with each other. Taken in the context of a known curse, they become part and parcel of a deliberate attempt to take revenge on those who have perpetrated a crime in the past and frequently on their descendants. It is with this very real objective in mind that the curse permeating the lives of one of Europe's most distinguished families is being spoken of in the present volume. Some members of that family may deny the existence of that curse, while the majority undoubtedly know nothing about it. Nevertheless, the curse is a reality; it has a basis in fact, and it has indeed found its mark.

The Curse of the Habsburgs

I had heard of the Habsburg curse ever since I was a little boy of 11. At that time, I had been to summer school in Vevey, Switzerland, and my father had sent for me to meet him in Zurich. One of the teachers was elected to accompany me on the train ride. I wasn't exactly his cup of tea. I had been a somewhat iconoclastic pupil during the past weeks, and I have a suspicion he was really glad to get rid of me, but nevertheless, it was going to be a long and hot train ride.

As we were passing through Aargau, the canton or province of Switzerland that lies roughly between Basle and Zurich, Monsieur Koehler, ever the teacher, grabbed my arm suddenly and pointed out the window. "See that castle over on the hill? That's the old Habsburg."

I looked, and in a fleeting glance observed a square tower rising on a hill not too far from the tracks. In a moment the train was past it.

Monsieur Koehler, who had not managed to make too deep an impression on me in class, now took the opportunity to shine before we parted company for good. "That castle is where the imperial Habsburgs come from," he explained, "but very few people realize it. What's more, did you know the castle is cursed?" I didn't, although, even at that age, my curiosity about such matters was aroused, but Monsieur Koehler knew very little more.

"*Habsburg* means Hawk Castle and the story goes that a man once lived there who was kind to the hawks that inhabited the grounds. But one day he did something terribly wrong, and the people of the land put a curse on him. Even his friends, the faithful hawks, left him. According to the story, he and all his descendants must suffer from the curse until the last one dies."

To an 11-year-old boy with a well-developed sense of imagination, this sounded like grist for my poetic mill. Had I not seen the actual publication of my first slender volume of poems (paid for by my Uncle Henry) only the winter before? The Habsburg saga was the stuff mysterious adventure stories are made of.

However, I forgot all about the incident until 40 years later. Again I was approaching the hill upon which the Habsburg stands. Only this time I had come on purpose, to check out the legendary Habsburg curse with the help of a renowned German psychic, Arthur Orlop, whom had come all the way from Mannheim to assist me in my quest.

A few months before my visit, the dimming memory of the Habsburg curse had been brought back to my attention while I was reading some popular magazines that dealt somewhat superficially with astrology, the occult, and parapsychology. In the magazine *Prediction*, I saw a two-paragraph mention of the ancient Habsburg curse. The story was simple enough: A reader was advising the editors of the existence of an authentic curse concerning the Habsburg family and castle. In essence, it was Monsieur Koehler's story except that, in this version, the hawks would leave when it was all over and done with. So long as a single hawk remained faithful to the Habsburg, the curse had not found its mark fully. But the story did not elaborate on the reasons for the curse nor did it give the name of the one who caused it.

On examining the historical evidence, we must not jump to the conclusion that every unfortunate event, every death, every political failure was due to a curse. With an ambitious family such as the Habsburgs, a number of successes and a number of failures are natural. It is only when the negative events take on a certain pattern, a certain repetition, or when the losses hint at the unexpected that we must take into consideration the possibility of a curse.

The house of Habsburgs, or, as it was later called, the house of Austria, certainly had many periods of great success. There is no denying that the Habsburgs frequently gained their objectives in world history, but curiously enough, in most cases, just after gaining some high plateau of success there came an unexpected, sudden reversal, as if the family was never to be left in a position to enjoy their triumphs for very long. The first time we can say with any degree of certainty that the curse became operative was in the life of Count Albert, the fourth Habsburg to bear this name.

From 1229 to 1239 the Holy Land was a quasi-European feudal kingdom where the crusaders lived off the land and enjoyed themselves immensely because there was very little warfare. During one of the main, unofficial border battles with raiding Arabs, Count Albert von Habsburg and his small band of knights were wiped out. The irony of this was that Count Albert had survived the major battles and was about to return home, when a routine patrol took his life. Still in his 20s, he had ruled over his lands a mere seven years.

During the ensuing centuries, the Habsburg rulers experienced one disaster after another: a defeat in battle, a nephew murdering his Imperial uncle, and the Swiss defeating their superior army and finally throwing the Habsburgs out of their native Switzerland for good. But it was not until 1848 and the revolutionary upheavals that shook Europe at that time, that a second curse hit home, and hit hard.

Centuries had passed since a young count Habsburg had raped a country girl, and a dismayed parent had uttered a curse that was to affect the Habsburg family for centuries to come. But the revolutionary events that tore Europe apart in 1848 also led to another even more powerful curse against the ruling member of the family, and one that ultimately led to their undoing.

The family was now the Habsburg-Lothringen, or Lorraine dynasty, as Maria Theresa had married Francis Stephen of Lorraine, and ruled jointly with him. But the old curse went right along, and the new one made things even worse.

It was during the period immediately following the putting down of the Hungarian revolt that another Habsburg curse originated. It was uttered by the mother of count Louis Batthyani, one of the Hungarian revolutionaries executed in 1849.

It appears that on August 27, 1849, a counsel of ministers met to divide the rebels into categories according to the severity of their offenses. A letter from General Haynau was read by the minister of justice, Dr. Schmerling, in which the general complained he was being hampered in the suppression of the Hungarian rebellion and in his just execution of the guilty. After much deliberation, General Haynau was given more or less free rein in dealing with the revolutionaries, and 13 generals were executed on October 6, 1849, bringing the total number of revolutionary leaders who had been executed to 19. Among those put to death was the prime minister of the Hungarian freedom government, count Louis Batthyani. His mother had submitted a request for an executive pardon to General Haynau, but her plea went unheeded, and her son was executed. It was when word reached her of his death that the curse was pronounced:

"May those responsible for the death of my son never have a happy day again in their lives. May he who ordered this execution be damned forever."

Although General Haynau had been given a free hand to execute the leaders, Francis Joseph (a direct descendent of the House of Habsburg-Lorraine) knew that Batthyani would be executed but did nothing to stop it. Surely the curse was meant for him above all others.

But the curses had not yet fully found their mark. In 1889, his only son and successor to be, Rudolph, who had openly defied his father and planned reforms for his future reign, was murdered by order of the Prime Minister, Count von Vetseram, together with his lover Mary Vetsera. A few years after that tragedy, Empress Elizabeth fell victim to an assassin's knife.

But it did not end there, either. Rudolph's replacement, Francis Ferdinand, got blown to pieces, with his wife, while visiting Bosnia, and the Sarajevo murders became the immediate reason for the start of World War I.

Only when Francis Joseph died in 1916, and the legendary blackbirds left the castle yards forever, did the curse exhaust itself.

PART FIVE:

The Nature of
Time and Space

CHAPTER 12
TIME AND SPACE

Most people are not even aware of the fact that time is called "the fourth dimension," because it defines a three-dimensional object's (or subject's) place in our time stream. Without these dimensions, we would not know when something were to occur. But that still does not tell us where the event will occur, until we know where it will be. Space is still another defining dimension.

The Other Side of Life, into which we all pass eventually, has three dimensions as do we—except that it is three-dimensional only to those living in it. When entities from the Other Side visit our physical world, they will appear to be two-dimensional images, unless they have fortified themselves by the temporary acquisition of denser matter called ectoplasm, from the solar plexus of the medium or sitters, in a séance.

In our physical world, we must have the three dimensions that define our appearance, plus the dimensions of time and space, sometimes called the time-space continuum.

One of the unsolved puzzles of mediumship is that mediums seem to be able to go beyond the limitations of these dimensions to bring us news of or information concerning events that either have not yet occurred, or which have already occurred but at a place seemingly inaccessible to the "psychic reporter," the medium. Actually, the so-called past and future are, in reality, an ongoing continuum, flow-ing *through* past, present, and future via "the eternal now." Thus fore-telling an event is really not violating any scientific principle or representing an exception from the system. There are no exceptions.

Psychics exercising their talents do not perform miracles; they simply make the firm laws of the universe work better for themselves than the average person can. Their talent and psychic ability allows them to use the system more extensively than others.

But even time and space are not wholly independent. Because it depends on the rotation of the planets around the sun, the time stream on Earth is different from the time on another planet. The Mars day is different from the Earth day.

Because of the relativity of time, depending where the observer is located, we may be told that a certain astral body is so many light years distant from us. If the double sun (star) called Zeta Reticuli II is 37.5 light years from us, that does not mean that a traveler from there to us would have to spend that many light years to reach us. If the traveler starts out from Zeta Reticuli II his journey to Earth would be based on their time stream, which may be entirely different from our time. Time is *not* absolute. Every planetary body has its own time, depending on the size of the planet, and the time it takes to move around its sun.

Zeta Reticuli II is a double sun, which complicates matters for the planet that circles them or at least one of them. A traveler from that system—the nearest to Earth that has planets—might also use an airship equipped with artificial magnetic fields, allowing it to set its own speed.

Space also depends on where the observer is located. But assum-ing the observer is on Earth, the distance of other space bodies will be correct as measured from Earth, but different if measured from some-where else.

In the universe, nothing is absolute. But because we, the observ-ers, live on Earth, the time-space continuum measured from here is applicable, always keeping in mind that other worlds may have differ-ent configurations as they travel from their world to ours.

Thus it may well be that even a planet circling a double sun 37.5 light years from us may allow its traveler to reach us in a much shorter period of *our time*.

Time Slips

When science fiction speaks of "time warps" and "time travel," we all know this is fiction, for our entertainment. But we do know of out-of-body experiences, where a person seemingly journeys by leaving the heavier physical body to other, actual places, observes people and things at that distant location, and then returns to the body, usually to wake up with the feeling of falling from a great height, as the respective "vibrations" (speeds) of travel are adjusted and the subject "slows down" psychically to be earthbound once more. OOBEs are a common psychic experience people have reported in large numbers. More often than not, experiences of this kind of astral projection include corroborative witnesses to back up the claim.

> *Mia Yamamoto, a Japanese-American woman living in New York City, was thinking of her sister in California one fine afternoon, when all of a sudden she felt herself shooting out of her body and within a moment—or what appeared to her almost instantaneously—she saw herself floating above her sister's house near Los Angeles. She noticed that her sister wore a certain green dress, and apparently her sister saw her too, for she waved up at her.*

> *The next moment, however, Mia was back in her body in New York. The experience so shook her up that she immediately wrote to her sister about it. But before that letter was even mailed, her sister called long distance to express her confusion at having observed Mia at her house in California and demanded an explanation!*

Now, mind you, this is not "distant viewing" or, as Eileen Garrett called it, "traveling clairvoyance" where the mind reaches out like a kind of radar to gather information. This is plain, simple astral projection of the inner body out of the physical body and then returning again to it.

What I am about to report has nothing to do with psychometry, the ability by many to relive the past through extrasensory perception. Psychometry is essentially a mental experience confined to the thought perception processes within the mind of the perceiver. It is a little like watching a movie inside your head. Perhaps more dramatic, but basically also two-dimensional is the ability of deep trance mediums to relive past events first person rather than by describing them.

Only when a deep trance medium is able to let an earthbound person—a ghost, if you will—speak through the medium's vocal apparatus, do we partake of a kind of living experience rather than a description of events past. Again, I am not about to report another ghost story of any kind.

What I am reporting here as the personal investigator of these amazing cases, is a rare and very puzzling phenomenon that does not fit into any of the aforementioned categories of psychic phenomena. It was *FATE* magazine that first called my attention to this sort of thing, by publishing the account of a gentleman in the Midwest and a town he visited, which does not seem to exist on the objective plane.

The *FATE* piece ran a good many years ago. Following that, on May 11, 1967, I was contacted by a reader of my books, Susan Hardwick of Philadelphia, Pennsylvania, who wanted to share an amazing experience with me in the hope of getting some explanations.

> "In the summer of 1960, I took a ride with a friend, Sal Sassani, along my favorite route. This was Route 152, starting in Philadelphia as Limekiln Pike, a beautiful, winding country road, which goes way up into the mountains. I have traveled it for years and knew every curve with eyes closed! About an hour after darkness fell, I sat stiff with a start: I knew we had not made an improper turn, yet the road was unfamiliar to me all of a sudden.
>
> "The trees were not the same. I became frightened and asked Sal to make a U-turn. As we did so, we both smelled what, to us, was like a combination of ether and alcohol. At the same time, the car radio fell silent! Suddenly we saw a shepherd puppy running alongside the car; his mouth was moving but no sound was heard! Then, from our right, where there was no real road, came a ghostly shadow of a long, hearse-like car. It crossed directly in front of us and disappeared. The odor vanished and the radio came back on at the same time."

I responded with questions, and on May 23, 1967, she contacted me again. To my question, whether she had ever had any other strange experience at that location, Susan Hardwick went on to report an earlier incident, which had apparently not been as frightening to her as the later one she'd first related.

> *"In the summer of 1958 I was driving with a friend, Jerry, on this same road, route 152, and we turned off it, onto New Galena Road. Halfway toward 611, which runs parallel to 152, we came upon a wooden building I had never seen there before. We stopped and entered and sat at a table, and my friend Jerry noticed a man who resembled his late father. We each had a Coke. This man addressed us both by our names, calling Jerry "son," and told him things only Jerry's father would have known. Jerry became convinced it was his father. We left and drove on a road I had never seen before, yet I knew exactly what lay around every bend and curve! The incident took place about an hour from the city; I know exactly where this spot is, but I have yet to see this structure or these roads again."*

I decided to go to Philadelphia with famed medium Sybil Leek and investigate the case.

On July 24, 1967, Sybil and I met up with Susan Hardwick, and a friend of hers, Barbara Heckner. I had told Ms. Leek nothing about the case, but as we were driving toward the area, I asked her if she received any kind of psychic impressions regarding it.

> *"This is not a ghostly phenomenon," she began, "this is a space phenomenon . . . we're going to cross a river."* We were approaching Lancaster, Pennsylvania, and there was no river in sight. Five minutes later, there was the river.

Sybil conveyed the feeling of masses of people in an open place, gathered for some reason, and she compared her feelings to an earlier visit to Runnymed, England, where people had once gathered to sign the Magna Carta.

Now we had reached the point 40 miles from Philadelphia, where Susan had been twice before and experienced the inexplicable. What did Sybil feel about the location?

> *"It's a happening . . . not a ghost . . . in the past . . . 200 years ago . . . out of context with time . . . I feel detached, like, no man's land . . . we shouldn't be here . . . as if we were aliens in this country . . . I have to think what day it is, why*

*we are here . . . it feels like falling off a cliff . . . I feel a large
number of people in a large open space."*

We began walking up an incline and Sybil indicated the vibrations
from the past were stronger there.

*"We are in their midst now, but these people are con-
fused, too. Why are they here?"*

"Unity . . . that is the word I get, unity."

I then turned to Susan Hardwick, and asked her to point out exactly where her two experiences had taken place. This was the first
time Sybil Leek heard about them in detail.

*"When I drove up here in 1958 with my friend, this road
we're on was not there, the road across from us was,
and there was a building here, a wooden frame building
that had never been there before. We felt somehow compelled to enter, and it seemed like a bar. We sat down
and ordered Cokes. There were several men in the place,
and my friend looked up and said, 'That man over there
looks like my father.' The man then spoke to us and called
us by our first names as if he knew us. He began predicting things about my friend's future and called him 'son.'"*

*"But didn't you think there was something peculiar about
all this?"*

*"Yes, of course we did, because Jerry's father had died
when he was a baby."*

"Did everything look solid to you?"

"Yes, very much so."

"How were the people dressed?"

"Country people . . . work shirts and pants."

"Were the Cokes you ordered . . . real?"

"Yes, real, modern Cokes."

*I looked around. There was nothing whatever in the area
remotely looking like a wooden building.*

"You're sure this is the spot, Susan?"

"Definitely, we used to picnic across the road . . . that little bridge over there is a good landmark."

"What happened then?"

"We finished our Cokes, walked out of the place, got into the car, and Jerry turned to me and said, 'That was my father.' He accepted this without any criticism. So we drove off and came upon a road that I had never seen before, and have yet to see again! I have tried, but never found that road again. Then I told Jerry to stop the car and told him, there would be a dilapidated farm building on the left, around the bend in the road. We proceeded to drive around it and sure enough, there it was. Then I stated there would be a lake on the right hand side . . . and there was, too."

"Did you ever find these places again?"

"Never. I am very familiar with the area . . . throughout my childhood I used to come here with friends many times."

"When you left the area, was there anything unusual in the atmosphere?"

"It felt rather humid . . . but it was an August afternoon."

"Did you go back later to try and find the place again?"
"Yes . . . we retraced our steps, but the building was gone. The road was still there, but no building."

"Was there anything in the atmosphere that was un-usual when you wandered into that wooden bar?"

"Humidity . . . an electrifying feeling. Very cool inside."

"The people?"

"The man who seemed to be Jerry's father, the bartender, and several other men sitting at the bar."

"Any writing?"

"Just signs like 'sandwiches' and different beer signs."

I thought about this for a while. Was it is all an hallucina-tion? A dream? A psychic impression? Susan assured me it was not: Both she and Jerry had experienced the same things, and neither of them had been asleep.

"What about the people you met inside this place? How did they look to you?"

"Solid, they walked . . . and . . . that was the funny thing . . . they all stared at us as if to say, who are you, and what are you doing here?"

"When you first drove up here and noticed that the area was unusual, did you notice any change from the normal road to this spot?"

"Only where the stop sign is now. That did not exist. Instead there was gravel and that wooden building. It started right in from the road, maybe 50 feet from the road. Further back it was as normal as it is today. Suddenly it was there, and the next moment we were in it."

I decided to go on to the second location, not far away, where Susan's other "time warp" experience had taken place in the summer of 1960. Again, as we approached it, I asked Sybil for any impressions she might have about the area and incident.

Even though this was a different location, though not too far from the other place, Sybil felt that "the strength of the force is constant" between the two places. But she did not feel any of the odd excitement she had earlier picked up on route to, and at the first location.

Once again, Susan pointed out the clump of trees she remembered from the incident.

"We were riding on this road," Susan explained, "a road, by the way, I have known for many years firsthand. It must have been around midnight, in the middle of July, in 1960. All of a sudden, this stretch of the road became extremely unfamiliar. The trees were not the same any more. They looked different, much older than they are now. There were no houses here, just completely open on the right side of the road." There were small houses in the area she pointed to. "This clump of trees was very thick, and out of there, where today there is no road, there was then a road. All of a sudden, on this road,

came a ghost car—like a black limousine, except that you could see through it."

At the same instant, she and her friend Sal saw a German shepherd puppy run alongside their car, with his mouth moving but without any sound, no barking being heard.

"How did the dog disappear?"

"He just ran off the road. When the black limousine pulled out in front of us and—a hearse I'd say. There is a cemetery right in back of us, you know."

There still is. But as Susan and Sal were driving in the opposite direction than the one they had come from, the hearse was going away from the cemetery, not toward it.

"What about the driver of the hearse?"

"Just a shadow. The hearse went alongside our car and then suddenly vanished. The whole episode took maybe seven or eight minutes. We drove back toward Philadelphia, very shook up."

Rather than drive on through the strange area of the road, they had decided to turn around and go back the other way.

Now it was our turn to turn around and head back to the city. For a while we sat silent, then I asked Sybil Leek to speak up if and when she felt she had something to contribute to the investigation.

"I think if you stayed in this area for a week, you wouldn't know what century you're in," she suddenly said, "I feel very confused . . . almost as if we had entered into another time, and then somebody pushes you back . . . as if they did not want you. This is a very rare situation . . . probably higher intensity of spiritual feeling. . . ."

I then turned to Susan's companion Barbara and asked her about her impressions, both now and before.

"An apprehensive kind of feeling came over me," she replied. "We were here a week and a half ago again, when we came upon this side of the road, and it was . . . different . . . it felt as if was not normal. All along this run, as soon as we hit 152, through New Galena, I feel as if I'm intruding . . . as

if I don't belong, as though this whole stretch of country were not in existence in my time. I've been out here hundreds of times and always had this odd sensation."

While neither Susan Hardwick nor her friends had ever attempted to research the past history of the peculiar area of their incidents, I of course did.

First I contacted the town clerk at Trambersville, Pennsylvania, today the nearest town to the area. Specifically, I wanted to know whether there ever was a village or a drugstore/bar/restaurant of some sort at the junction of Highway 152 and New Galena Road, not far from the little bridge, which is still there. Also, I asked to know something of the history of the area.

The reply came on March 1, 1968, from the director of the Bucks County Historical-Tourist Commission in Fallsington, Pennsylvania.

"It is rural farm area now and has been from the beginning. From what I know about this area, and from *Place Names in Bucks County* by George MacReynolds, and Davis's *Story of Bucks County*, I know nothing of a drugstore in the area."

There was something else: Susan Hardwick reported finding some strange holes in the road in the area. "They seemed like they were left from the snow . . . filled with water . . . like a whirlpool. Many times we stopped our car and put our hands into those potholes and *we could not feel the road underneath them.* My friends and I stuck our arms into the holes and got wet. There was water in them. But when we came back another time, there were no holes. No water. Nothing."

This got me thinking to search further in George MacReynolds' excellent work, *Place Names in Bucks County*, which also contains the detailed biography of the area.

And here is where I found at least a partial explanation for what these people had experienced along New Galena Road.

It appears that back in the 1860s galena (and lead) ore was discovered in this area, and mines were started. Soon there was a veritable mini "gold rush" for lead and some silver also, and people in the farm area began driving shafts into the earth to see if there was valuable ore underneath. Those must have been the deep, bottomless "potholes" with water in them that Susan and her friends rediscovered— or at least their imprints from the past of New Galena.

The town of New Galena became a mining center. Mining fever hit the rural population and turned farmers into speculators. By 1874 it was all over, though another attempt at exploiting the mines in the area was made in 1891 and as late as 1932 some work to restore railroad tracks to the mines was done: but it all came to naught. "Today the place is deserted," writes MacReynolds, "a ghost of itself in the boom days of the 60s and 70s."

This explains the strange feeling of not wanting "outsiders" intruding into their own mining bonanza, and it explains the water-filled shafts in the road. What it fails to explain is Jerry's father and the Coke bottles Susan Hardwick and Jerry drank from.

I can only suggest that so intense an emotional fervor as that of a small, rural community suddenly caught up in a mining fever and dreams of great riches, might create a kind of psychic bubble in which it continues to exist in a time-space continuum of its own, separate from the outside world, except for occasional, accidental intruders, such as Susan and her friends.

While these kinds of experiences are rare, they are by no means unique. Somewhat similar is a case reported to me by Mrs. Rebecca B., who also lives in the Philadelphia area.

"My husband and I were traveling on River Road from Route 611, on our way to the Poconos. We should have been in the Easton area when we 'hit the curve,' but we were not. I knew the trip by heart because I had been going that route since infancy to visit my grandfather. Over the years, despite storms and floods, much of the landscape and housing was the same.

"Yet on this trip, all of a sudden we found ourselves in this very strange place. We stopped. Across the street was an old saloon made of wood, the doors wide open, with darkness inside. The sidewalk was not of cement but rather a raised wooden sidewalk unlike anything we had ever seen outside of old movies. The people standing in front of the saloon were wearing work clothes, jeans, flannel shirts, Stetson type hats, and there was a dog and a couple men standing and one sitting on the 'porch,' his feet dangling down. One woman with a

Grapes of Wrath–*type cotton dress was there also. Everything seemed covered with dust—building, shoes— earthy dust, not coal dust.*

"There was nobody on the road except my husband and I, and the townspeople stood and stared at us also with a haunting look, as if to say, 'what the hell are you doing here?'

"We felt unsafe and not in the right place, and decided to drive off. The road was like a dirt road, bumpy and rutted with a dust effect not seen anywhere else on our journey. The incident happened in broad daylight, there were no other vehicles around (which is strange) . . . and there was no sound at all."

◆—◆ ⊨◇⊨ ◆—◆

About the same time, I heard of a parallel case through the late Ethel Johnson Meyers, the famed trance medium and psychic reader. A friend of hers in California had communicated to her an extraordinary experience that she felt was so unusual, I had better investigate myself.

Waylaid in Another Time

On June 1, 1967, I sat opposite Robert Cory, designer and actor, living then on Elmwood Street in Burbank. At the time Mr. Cory was 30 years old and premonitions and dreams were accepted phenomena in his family, which was of Near Eastern extraction.

In 1964, Cory took a vacation trip by car to visit his future in-laws in Kenwick, Washington. His fiancé was with him, and he left her with her parents after a few days, to drive back to Burbank by himself. His car was a '57 Corvette, in excellent condition, and Mr. Cory was an experienced driver. The fall weather was dry and pleasant when he left Washington state. It would be a 12-hour trip down to the Los Angeles area.

Cory left Washington around 11:30 p.m., and when he crossed the Oregon state line it was already dark. The weather had not changed, however. He started to climb up into the mountains on a long, winding road south. About four hours after he left Washington, around 3:30 a.m., he was rounding a bend, and with one fell swoop he found himself in a snowstorm. One moment it was a clear, dry autumn night, the next, a raging snowstorm. It was unbelievable.

"I slowed down, I was frightened, " he explained, still shuddering at the experience now. "The road was narrow, with mountain on one side and a drop on the other."

Cory got out of the car; he could drive no further. It was ice cold and snowing. Then he saw in the distance what appeared to be a bright light, so he got back into the car and drove on.

When he got to "the light" it turned out to be a road sign, reflecting light "from somewhere." But he was now on top of a hill, so he coasted downhill until the car came to a full stop. Cory looked out and discovered he had rolled into some sort of village, for he saw houses and when he got out of the car, he found himself on a bumpy street.

"What did this town look like?" I asked.

"It looked like a Western town; the road went through it, but the road now had bumps in it, as if it were a road with much work done to it."

Cory found the car would not go any further anyway, and he was glad to be in this strange place. One building had the word "hotel" on it, and he walked toward it on wooden sidewalks. He knocked at the door, everything was dark. But the door was open and he found himself in the lobby of the hotel. He yelled for someone to come, but nobody came—yet there was a potbellied stove with a fire in it, and he placed himself in front of it to get warm. To one side he noticed a barbershop chair, and in the back, a desk and a big clock. To his left, he saw what looked to him like a phone booth. It turned out this was an ancient telephone you had to crank to get action. He cranked it and cranked it, but the noise worried him, so he took off his sweater and wrapped it around the box while cranking to keep the noise down. But nobody answered.

"So what did you do next?"

"I went back to the stove, ready to go to sleep and maybe in the morning there would be somebody there to talk to. After all, they've got a fire going: there must be some life in the place. So I lay down on a sofa, when I heard a rattling noise coming from what looked like a cardboard box in a corner. I figured it might be a snake and got real worried.

"The heat was putting me to sleep, I was exhausted and so I just fell asleep. I woke up due to some sound upstairs, and I saw a man coming down the steps, an old man of maybe 75, wearing big boots, which made the noise."

"What did he look like?"

"He wore old coveralls, like a farmer. Slowly he came down and to where the stove was, he sat down in a rocking chair across from it, and then he went to the men's room, or something, and again sat down. He saw me, and we nodded to each other. Then he kept on rocking while I was trying to get up courage to ask him some questions. Finally he said to me, 'You couldn't fall asleep . . . why don't you fall asleep?' I said, 'Well, that's alright, I'm not really tired, you know,' but he replied, 'No, you couldn't fall asleep, it's okay, it's okay.'"

"How did his voice sound?"

"Like an old man's voice, and as he kept saying over and over again, 'It's okay,' I fell asleep again. Once or twice I opened my eyes and saw him still sitting there. I slept till daybreak, and when I woke up and opened my eyes, I saw eight or 10 men walking around, talking, doing different things. I sat up but no one paid attention to me. As if I were not there. But I got up and said hello to one of them, and he said hello back to me; there were a couple men around the stove with their backs to me, talking, and then there was a man standing behind the barber chair shaving somebody who wasn't even there."

"Exactly what did you see?"

"He was shaving somebody, talking to him, moving his razor—but there was no one in that chair. He held up the invisible chin and carefully wiped the razor into paper. It was frightening to watch this. The razor was real alright."

"Was there anything unusual about these people?"

"They seemed like normal people, except I had the feeling they were in some way smaller. They all looked very old, like the first man I saw coming down the stairs."

"What happened next?"

"One of the men was walking back and forth in the hotel lobby, talking to nobody, arguing, carrying on a conversation all by himself. So I got up finally and looked outside, my car was still there, and the snow had stopped. There was no sign of life outside. I turned to the three men around the stove and asked, 'Is there a gas station around?' Now I could understand they were speaking to me but the words made no sense. One of the men grabbed my wrist as if to point out a direction. Then I heard someone yell out 'breakfast.' I looked and noticed in the back of the lobby where the desk was, two doors were open now, leading into a dining room. Again the voice yelled, 'breakfast, come, breakfast,' and this time the old man, the one I had seen first coming down the stairs, came over and grabbed my arm, saying, 'come have breakfast.'

"I became so frightened I backed off and for the first time raised my voice, saying 'No, thank you.' Everybody turned around and then they started to walk toward me, slowly, normally, not rushing. I said, 'Where am I? Where am I?' and the old man, who still held my arm, said, 'don't worry, don't worry,' but I turned and walked out and got into my car. I had forgotten about running out of gas."

"Did it work?"

"Yes it did. I drove down this bumpy road and the faces of the men looking out of the windows of the hotel behind me."

"Did you get a good look at these people? What did they look like?"

"Normal."

"You say he actually touched you? Did you feel it?"

"Yes, I certainly did."

"The clothes these people wore . . . were they of our time?"

"No, no. When I drove off, I saw some more people in the street, one of them a woman, she wore a long dress like the Salvation Army women do."

"Describe what happened then as you left the place."

"I drove past the people on the sidewalk, and then there was something like a cloud I went through—like a fog— for about 30 seconds . . . next thing I knew, I came out into one of the brightest, shiniest days you could imagine. I drove another half a mile or so until I saw a gas station, just in time. I was back in today's life."

"Did you question him about the place you had just left?"

"Here I was with a sweater, all buttoned up, and the attendant in short sleeves, bare chest out, sweating, and he gave me a funny look. I just couldn't tell him, no."

"Was there anything different about the atmosphere in that place you left?"

"Yes; I was very tense and nervous. But I was not dreaming this, I touched the sofa, I was fully awake."

At that point, Cory contacted his old friend Ethel Meyers and wrote down his experience for her, and she in turn called me.

I then looked at his original report to Ethel Meyers, and realized he had left out some details when we met for the interview, three years later. Important details. Here they are:

When Cory arrived at the "hotel", there were 6–8 inches of snow outside. He noticed wagons parked outside the *hotel, wagons that hitch on to horses! He found this peculiar in this age.*

When he entered the lobby and looked around for the first time, Cory noticed animal heads on the walls, old furniture of another era, and a calendar on the wall dating back to dates in the late 1800s. The telephone had a sign reading CRANK BOX FOR OPERATOR. There was a clock on the wall ticking loud. There were cats in one of the chairs, kittens to be exact.

Apparently, there was more conversation between Cory and the old man. "Nice day isn't it?" he said and put his hand on Cory's shoulder. It felt more like "a chicken's foot."

Finally, when Cory drove off and looked back at the faces of the men in the hotel, pressed against the windows, he clearly noticed tears rolling down the face of "his" old man . . . seeing him leave.

Clearly, this is neither an imprint from the past nor an hallucination or ghostly apparition, as we know them. The fog Cory drove through on his way "out" reminds me of the fog sometimes reported by people abducted by UFOs, or in connection with their landings. What have we here? I can only guess that somehow the combined energies of the people Cory encountered were strong enough, and their fear of leaving their little world powerful enough, to create this enclave in our time stream, forever keeping them from going on.

A Long Journey Down Under

When I first wrote of the "time travel" experiences of two Pennsylvania women in a magazine devoted to psychical research, I was contacted shortly after its publication by a woman in far away Australia—Mrs. Anita Stapleton of Labrador, Queensland—who wanted me to investigate a somewhat similar incident in the life of a close friend. Rather than have her very lucid account of what he told her, I asked to speak to the gentleman directly, and so it was that on May 5, 1991, Mr. Kenneth B. Burnett, of Southport, Queensland, got in touch with me.

Mr. Burnett is a man of many talents, and keen observation. He has spent most of his adult rife in a variety of jobs, ranging from that of a ceramic tile salesman to lumberjack, from steelwork painter to private detective. At age 58, he was forced to retire on a pension due to a physical condition brought on eventually by his war service. He has "all kinds of diseases," as he puts it, but never lost his sense of humor. His heart condition does prevent him from running around too much, but despite his afflictions, he really seems quite fit. Among his other talents, now that he has the time to indulge it, is the making of custom knives, a gift his son has also inherited to good advantage.

"So you see, " Burnett says, "I'm just an average, everyday sort of chap."

Quite so.

His strange adventure occurred in the northern part of New South Wales, on the east coast of Australia, in 1968, when Burnett and his wife Meg decided to visit Meg's brother in Armidale, 70 miles distant from where they lived at that time. They knew the area like the back of their hands. Ken was an excellent driver, and his car was a Toyota station wagon. I asked for his initial report, which he had jotted down previously, in his own words.

"In 1968, Meg and I decided to drive from Katoomba to her brother's house in Armidale. We traveled via the Mitchell and the Oxley Highways. It was a cold, snowy winter. We spent the first night sleeping in the back of our Toyota Station Wagon at the outskirts of Dubbo. It was so cold that eventually we set off at a very early hour, and still dark, to complete our journey to Armidale. While driving, the car heater was a boon!

"From memory, we were driving along on a mountainous, twisting road, hills or cliffs on one side, and sheer drop on the passenger's side, the edge clearly marked by a white painted railing all the way. On several occasions, approaching bends, the lights failed completely and it was only my ability to retain a mental "picture" of where the fence had been that enabled me each time to stop safely and search for the fault. When the lights came on again each time, we would set off again until the next time. It became really hair-raising. When we stopped at Tamworth for fuel at an overnight petrol station, I made a real hunt for the lighting fault but could not

find anything that I could definitely say had been the problem. As it was dawn I did not worry any further.

"Shortly after leaving Tamworth, and near Moonbi, we came to a point on the highway where detour signs directed us off into the bush on the right. After about 200 yards I noticed that there were other tire marks on this track. That made me uneasy. After about another 200 yards the track narrowed to one car's width and the ground suddenly dropped away on each side, making me even more uneasy because if another vehicle came towards us it would not have been possible for either vehicle to move forward and pass. We were traveling then on a sort of whitish chalk base and each side of the road or track accommodated very spindly trees which appeared to be mainly Ash or Aspen. We were a long time on this track and must have driven about 10 hair-raising miles when we came to a tunnel. This was no wider than the track and convinced me that we were on some sort of old and disused railway track, although there was not the slightest sign that a track had ever been laid on it. The tunnel proved to be about half a mile in length, but due to the extreme narrowness, seemed much more.

"When we came out of the tunnel, the track gradually became wider until, after about a mile, was almost wide enough for two vehicles to pass each other if driven by experienced and careful drivers. We must have driven another 10 miles, at least, until we came to a bituminized highway and opposite the outlet of our track was a very poor road sign showing Walcha to the right and Armidale to the left. We turned left and after a while reached Bendemeer where a road sign said that Armidale was to our right. I turned right and eventually reached our relative's house in Armidale. They were extremely worried about our being so late and it turned out that we had taken all of a very full day to drive from Tamworth to Armidale, a distance of 70 miles! Where had we been? My brother-in-law assured me that the highway from Tamworth to Armidale was an excellent one and there

*had been no roadwork, and certainly no Detour sign there
for years.*

*"The track I described, and particularly the tunnel, sim-
ply have never existed in the area, due to the terrain,
there is no ground suitable for such a track to have ever
been built."*

While the report stressed the salient points of the events, there
were some unanswered questions I put to Mr. Burnett, especially in
respect to his feelings, sensations, and anything out of the ordinary
suggesting a strange phenomenon.

For one thing, Burnett thought that the whole thing was due to
some mysterious "evil force" or spirit trying to harm them, though I
must confess I have not found this to be so from the evidence I have.
However, Mr. Burnett (and his family) have had true psychic experiences for many years and his gift of ESP may have some bearing on
the case. In answer to my new questions, he wrote:

*"I will do my best to describe my sensations at the time
of the trip. I had put the problem of the car's lighting
problems down to being 'just one of those things' until
later events convince me that it was otherwise.*

*"The lights only failed at highly dangerous parts of a
mountain road, and on curves where only an expert driver
could hope to avoid an accident of some sort.*

*"When the detour signs showed up, I turned off the road
onto an area about 60 feet wide by 40 feet deep, which
acted as a sort of foyer at the beginning of the chalk
road. I first felt nervy here, because as I left the bitumen
of the highway, I could see that no other vehicle had
used this detour before, and that the ground was covered with a thick carpeting of Autumn leaves from Aspen trees. Only Australian timbers grow in the area
concerned and I was further disturbed and alerted when
I found that the narrow chalk road was lined very neatly
on each side by Aspen trees, all in Autumn leaf. We were
driving in winter for one thing, and for another thing, there
are no Aspen trees in the area.*

"My wife had felt extremely uneasy all along, but could not explain why, because she has always had complete confidence in my driving ability.

"My nerve ends tingled again as we approached the old road sign as we were leaving the chalk track. We had come to a cross road, in very bad repair, and looking at us was a positively ancient and bleached road sign with barely legible printing on it directing us to Armidale on the left. The wood of that sign was bleached gray with age and badly weathered and cracked. No Council would have left it in that state.

"The country surrounding Armidale is very mountainous, and there is simply nowhere such a long track and tunnel could exist either then or in the past! I am convinced that such a road did not ever exist in that area. The only trees on the edge of that road were Aspen. Not even one Aussie tree anywhere in sight! That made me feel queerer than anything else at the time, actually, because while we drove on that road I had a strange feeling of unreality and timelessness! The tunnel was cut right through a mountain of sandstone and the rocks of that area are all granite conglomerates.

"The biggest shock of all, to an experienced long-distance driver, was the taking of something like 12 hours to cover a distance of 70 miles! Simply not possible!

"On my return trip my wife and I took particular care in looking for the spot where we had been detoured off the highway. Such a spot simply did not exist. Also, just as my brother-in-law had stated, the highway between Armidale and Tamworth was in superb condition!

"Two or three years after that incident, I was able to learn from a friend of Anita Stapleton's, who had an uncle who had worked on the Railways in that area for more than 40 years, that nowhere in that area could a track or tunnel so long have possibly existed now or in the past and, although some narrow tracks had existed in the Cobb & Co. coach days, none of them was chalk, *and there were no known tunnels of any kind anywhere in the area. They simply did not exist.*

"I still do not know how we could just 'disappear' for about 12 hours on a main highway in broad daylight, which it was when I left Tamworth for Armidale. Had we simply sat at the side of the road, somebody would most certainly have stopped to offer help and at least one Police Patrol would also have wanted to know why we were stopped.

"It remains the greatest mystery of my life and I am no stranger to mysteries!"

In longhand, Burnett added to his report. "What could be an important omission is the fact that whilst on the chalk road, I noticed that the trees along the sides of the road did not throw a shadow, and they should have done."

Once again, I asked Burnett for further data: Did such a tunnel and road exist somewhere else perhaps? There was also the tantalizing possibility of an UFO abduction to account for the lost time. Did he and his wife observe any UFOs in the area at the time?

Mr. Burnett was very cooperative. He contacted the Tamworth Historical Society on December 11, 1991, in respect to information about the road, and the trees in the area, Elder or Ash or even Popular. To his surprise, the answer came back quickly, and Arthur Maunder, the research officer of the Society, confirmed both road and trees as really in existence, which does not really solve the puzzle at all.

How and why did Burnett drive so far off his goal? How was it that on a road he knew well, he suddenly saw a detour sign that did exist, but at a distance? And what made him lose 12 hours?

My guess is that the road and trees, though still in existence, appeared to the Burnetts in an earlier time—remember that the Burnetts did not see any road beyond the detour sign, only the "track" they were forced to take because of it. What caused him to leave the present and make a detour into what appears to be the past? My inclination is to involve his known psychic abilities. Did he, for a time, become a vehicle for a spirit entity, or was he guided by one to go off the intended road for some reason?

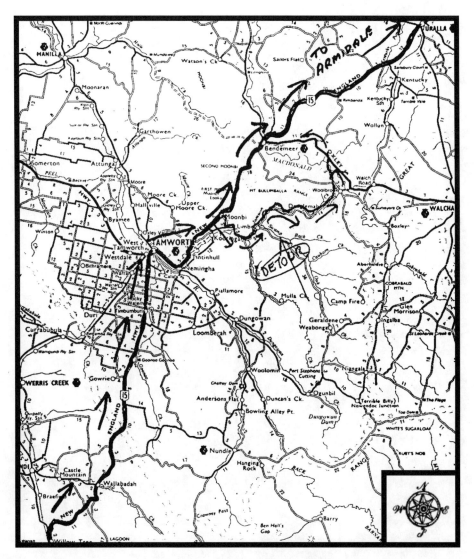

A Long Journey Down Under

PART SIX:

Path to the Truth

CHAPTER 13
THE REAL ALCHEMY

Whenever anyone talks about "alchemy" or "alchemists," pictures of little men desperately trying to make artificial gold for powerful rulers come to mind. That is the image the average person has of the art of alchemy, and it is a false one.

To begin with, the term, derived from the Arabic, refers to the ability to change things (not necessarily only metal), and became the word *chemistry* in today's sense. But even that modern term frequently has other connotations than the purely mechanistic one, such as in "the right chemistry between people." Of course, tourists visiting the castle mount at Prague, Czechoslovakia, are always proudly shown the Goldmakers' Lane, where Emperor-King Rudolph II kept his gold-making adepts occupied round the clock to make gold—or so the tourist guides tell you. But even that isn't true, or rather, it is only partially so. What exactly *is* alchemy then?

The great Swiss Physician and philosopher Theophrastus Paracelsus believed that the true purpose of alchemy was not to make gold cheaply, but to find a panacea to cure all ills, both of the body and the mind. Paracelsus wisely left the cure of the soul to the professional religionists—after all, he lived in an age when the wrong religious statement could cost one his life. But even Paracelsus, a truly modern thinking man of the 16th century, was fascinated by the laboratory aspects and possibilities of "the art."

Although the world of the Renaissance had dubbed alchemy "the Royal Art" for obvious reasons (what could be more desirable than making gold, both the metal and the human gold of wisdom?), Paracelsus referred to it as the *spagyric* art, a word he himself had invented meaning "to part and to unite."

The mysterious *philosopher's stone*, the core of the alchemical search, without which nothing could be accomplished, was to be obtained solely from natural sources! Secrecy was vital for those who were to become the experts, the "adepts," but of course not everyone was so qualified. "If you are ignorant of the customs of Cabalists and astrologers," Paracelsus wrote, "God did not select you for the spagyric art or nature for metallurgy, not should you be told anything about alchemy."

It all started in ancient Egypt where, because it was the color of the sun—the Egyptian's supreme object of worship—gold was kept in highest esteem. The sun was sacred and so was gold. The Greek philosopher Aristotle thought that all substances in existence were only variations of gold, which he called "the prime matter." Therefore changing other matters into gold was indeed possible, at least in theory. Notice how close this concept comes to Einstein's Unified Field Theory and our increasing conviction that all matter and energy are one!

In Alexandria, Egypt, a great center of learning during the first Christian century, the Gnostics, a mixture of Pagan and Judeo-Christian philosophers, developed the former purely chemical quest for gold into the more philosophical realm of human elevation and change. From then on, alchemy had a dual purpose: making gold from baser elements (to show mastery over matter) and making man perfect by eliminating his faults (to show mastery of spirit).

Material alchemy calls for laboratory equipment, fires, elixirs, and chemical substances, which are applied one to the other in extremely concise and specific ways, essentially a continuing process of dissolving and recapturing substances which are alternately heated and cooled to obtain the desired change.

Spiritual alchemy, on the other hand, calls for better understanding of man's desires, man's destiny, through the inner meanings of words, symbols, numbers, sounds and even colors—the understanding of what we understand under esoteric magic (not stage magic of course).

In this quest, alchemists always considered their "bible" the alleged writings of a mysterious personage called Hermes Trismegistus, or "thrice greatest Hermes." He is the acknowledged author of a set of "emerald tablets" allegedly found in the Great Pyramid of Cheops (but of course nowhere to be seen today).

Notice that the notion of sacred magical tablets is by no means unique: Moses had a set, and even as recently as the Mormon revelation to Joseph Smith in New York state, we hear of golden tablets with a special message on them (which have since disappeared, we are also told). Could this tablet story have symbolic meaning rather than tangible significance?

At any rate, Hermes the great teacher says, "It is true without doubt and certain: The nether is like the upper and the upper is like the nether, to accomplish the wonders of the one and even as all things arose from the word of the one so likewise shall all things by virtue of aggregation be born of the one." (The simplified essence of this speech is widely quoted as the adage "as above, so below.") And he goes on to explain, in symbolic terms, so the layman is suitably confused as to their meaning, how the power to accomplish "the great work" (alchemy's term for transmutation) is accomplished.

"Separate earth from fire, the fine from the coarse, gently and with great sagacity. It ascends from Earth to heaven and down again to Earth, to receive the power of the upper and of the nether. Thus you shall call the glorious light of the world your own, and all darkness shall fall away from you." What Hermes says is that heaven and Earth are interrelated, and Earth was created in the image of heaven!

If we were to discover God's system in creating our world, we then would be able to reorganize it. "I am called Hermes the thrice greatest, because I possess the three parts of wisdom of the universe," wrote Hermes. And, what are these parts? They are the aspects represented by sun, moon, and man's ingenuity. Democrit, the author of *Physica et Mystica,* added that the key to this work was a "stone which carries within itself the seeds of the two precious metals, capable of reproducing them, called The Philosophers' Stone."

Notice how close the idea of *seeds* of metals comes to modern concepts of atomic physics? But just as refinement of metal yields a finer form of metal, so the inner meanings of alchemy are handed down by priests in a hermetic (that is, closed) chain excluding outsiders. That hermetically sealed "vessel" is man. If gold is a living thing containing a seed, it can be made to grow by the application of certain substances. The main "medicine" to accomplish this is called the Elixir or Philosopher Stone.

The process of turning "ignoble" metal (usually lead or mercury) into a "noble" metal (gold or sometimes silver) is relatively simple: The base substance is brought in contact with the Elixir (the term used in alchemy is *projection*), and as a result of the contact, the base substance turns into gold or silver. Thirty years ago, such a notion was called a medieval fantasy. Today we know very well that it takes only a minor adjustment in the atom of lead to turn it into gold. Unfortunately, while we are technically able to do this, the cost of the undertaking far outweighs the results. But it proves that the alchemists of old really did know exactly what had to be done to obtain the transmutation in metals.

As to the more complex problem of human change, they were even more adept: they realized that only a full understanding of nature and universal law would allow man to fulfill his proper destiny and reach out to greater knowledge, greater ability to perform his role. One must, however, realize that they found this to be so at a time when the Church was still very powerful and viewed such opinions as heresies. Nothing retards human progress more than dogmatic religion, and if anyone really wishes to pinpoint the role of "the devil" on Earth, let him find him in the persona of the religious establishment. Despite this danger, alchemy penetrated into many levels of society, and the wise men *knew* the real truth about themselves, about what we call today psychology, and even some of the true aspects of the universe at a time when official Church doctrine held the Earth to be the center of the universe!

Alchemy, then, far from being the expression of greed for cheap gold, was (and is) the quest to turn the human dross of greed, evil thought, selfishness, and hatred into the "gold" of love, spiritual enfoldment oneness with the God within *and* without, and the rhythm of nature, a world from which man has so alienated himself for far too long. The way back is by no means easy, but neither is it obstructed (in this truly "unobstructed universe") if we understand the central theme.

"As above, so below," the basic message of Hermes the thrice greatest, points the way to mining the richest mine of all, our own human *soul*.

FURTHER READING

For those who are interested in further study of some of the topics raised in this book, I have prepared a list of titles, arranged by subject, that may prove interesting.

The Psychic

Holzer, Hans. *The Psychic Yellow Pages*: Kensington/Citadel.

Prophecy

Nostradamus

No other prophet attracted as much attention among the broad masses as did this great prophet of the 16th century.

One should, however, study these books with a measure of caution. The original text is reliable, all right, but the translations from 16th-century French are not always correct, as the French of his time and modern French often differ in meaning. Further, as Stuart Robb has pointed out, certain terms had specific meaning to Nostradamus, but may have a different meaning to anyone else at the same period.

For instance, when Nostradamus speaks of "oriental," he does not mean "Asian," but simply a "person from the East"—east of France, that is.

As mentioned elsewhere in this text, I consider the most accurate books on Nostradamus to be Stuart Robb's.

Cheetham, Erika. *The Prophecies of Nostradamus.*

Cheetham, Erica. *The Further Prophecies of Nostradamus:1985 and Beyond.*

Drude, Karl. *Nostradamus.* (In German.)

Hogue, John. *Nostradamus and the Millennium.* (Excellent, visual.)

Hogue, John. *The Millennium Book of Prophecy*: HarperCollins. (Even better than his first book.)

MacHovec, Frank J. *Nostradamus: His Prophecies for the Future.*

Putzien, Rudolph. N*ostradamus—Weissagungenueber den Atomkrieg.* (German.)

Robb, Stuart. *Nostradamus and the Ends of Evils Began*: Long Meadow Press. (Excellent, perhaps the best.)

Robb, Stuart. *Nostradamus and Napoleon.*

Robb, Stuart. *Prophecies on World Events by Nostradamus.*

Roberts, Henry. *The Complete Prophecies of Nostradamus.* (A Controversial text.)

Ward, Charles A. *Oracles of Nostradamus.* (This is a very old book.)

Edgar Cayce

Cerminara, Gina. *Many Mansions,* 1950.

Kirkpatrick, Sidney. *Edgar Cayce: An American Prophet*: Putnam, 2000.

Stearn, Jess. *The Sleeping Prophet*: Bantam Books, 1967.

Sugrue, Thomas. *There Is A River,* 1942.

Psychic Healing

Holzer, Hans. *The Secret of Healing*: Beyond Words Publishers. (The true story of the healing powers of Ze'ev Kolman.)

Channeling

Klimo, Jon. *Channeling*: Jeremy Tarcher.

The Other Side

Holzer, Hans. *Life Beyond*: Contemporary Books, 1994.

Solomon, Philip, and Hans Holzer. *Beyond Death: Conditions in the Afterlife*: Hampton Roads, 2001.

Swedenborg, Emanuel. *Heaven and Hell*.

Ghosts

Holzer, Hans. *Ghosts*: Black Dog & Levanthal, 2000.

INDEX

ABOUT THE AUTHOR

Professor Hans Holzer, Ph.D., taught parapsychology for eight years at the New York Institute of Technology and lectures widely. He has written 135 published books, including *Life Beyond*; *Ghosts*; *The Alchemist*; *Are You Psychic?*; and *Beyond Death: Conditions in the Afterlife*. Dr. Holzer has written and produced a number of television documentaries, including "This House is Haunted," and a number of segments for the seminal TV series *In Search Of...*

Dr. Holzer studied at the University of Vienna, Austria; at Columbia University, New York, and received his doctorate from the London College of Applied Science. He also has a Master's degree in Comparative Religion. He is a member of the Writer's Guild of America, the Author's Guild, Producer's Guild, AFTRA, SAG, and ASCAP. He lives and works in New York.

Other Books by Hans Holzer

Ghosts	Black Dog & Levanthal
Witches	Black Dog & Levanthal
The Lively Ghosts of Ireland	Barnes & Noble
Ghosts of New England	Random House
Are You Psychic?	Putnam
Hans Holzer's Psychic Yellow Pages	Kensington Books
Where The Ghosts Are	Kensington Books
More Where The Ghosts Are	Kensington Books
Life Beyond	Contemporary Books of Chicago
Hans Holzer's Haunted America	Barnes & Noble
Great American Ghost Stories	Barnes & Noble
Real Hauntings	Barnes & Noble
True Ghost Stories	Barnes & Noble
Window to the Past	Kensington Books
The Psychic Side of Dreams	Llewellyn
Elvis Speaks from the Beyond	Random House
The Secrets of Healing	Beyond Words